CASEBOOK on
CORPORATE GOVERNANCE and
MANAGEMENT PRACTICES
in Pakistani Organizations

CASEBOOK on CORPORATE GOVERNANCE and MANAGEMENT PRACTICES
in Pakistani Organizations

MUNTAZAR BASHIR AHMED

OXFORD
UNIVERSITY PRESS

OXFORD
UNIVERSITY PRESS

Oxford University Press is a department of the University of Oxford.
It furthers the University's objective of excellence in research, scholarship,
and education by publishing worldwide. Oxford is a registered trade mark of
Oxford University Press in the UK and in certain other countries

Published in Pakistan by
Ameena Saiyid, Oxford University Press
No.38, Sector 15, Korangi Industrial Area,
PO Box 8214, Karachi-74900, Pakistan

ISBN 978-0-19-940549-7

Typeset in Adobe Garamond Pro
Printed on 70gsm Imported Offset Paper

Printed by The Times Press Pvt. Ltd., Karachi

CONTENTS

AFF	A. F. Ferguson & Company
ARL	Attock Refinery Limited
CSIBL	Crescent Standard Investment Bank Limited
CSBM	Crescent Business Management Services Limited
CTTL	Callmate Telips Telecom Limited
CEO	Chief Executive Officer
CFO	Chief Financial Officer
CIO	Chief Information Officer
DPS	Dividend per share
DRP	Disaster Recovery Plan
ECPL	Engro Chemical Pakistan Ltd.
EPS	Earnings per share
ERP	Enterprise Resource Planning
EVTL	Engro Vopak Terminal Ltd
FATA	Federally Administered Tribal Areas
FDD	Functional Design Document
FSIBL	First Standard Investment Bank Limited
FLCL	First Leasing Corporation Limited
FPLC	First Paramount Leasing Company
HSD	High Speed Diesel
IFC	International Finance Corporation
IHFL	International Housing Finance Limited
ISP	Internet Service Provider
IPP	Independent Power Plant
JESCO	Jhang Electric Supply Corporation
KESC	Karachi Electric Supply Company
KIBOR	Karachi Inter Bank Offer Rate
KAPCO	Kot Addu Power Company
KSE	Karachi Stock Exchange
MP&NR	Ministry of Petroleum & Natural Resources
MMS	Material Management System

MRCS	Material Requirements Costing System
NBFC	Non-Bank Financial Company
NRL	National Refinery Limited
OMC	Oil Marketing Company
OGDC	Oil and Gas Development Corporation
OGRA	Oil and Gas Regulatory Authority
OIBPL	Orix Investment Bank Pakistan Limited
PACRA	Pakistan Credit Rating Agency
PAEC	Pakistan Atomic Energy Commission
PARCO	Pak Arab Refinery Company
PEL	Pak Elektron Limited
PICIC	Pakistan Industrial Credit Investment Corporation
PLL	Paramount Leasing Limited
PLCL	Pacific Leasing Company Limited
PRL	Pakistan Refinery Limited
PEPCO	Pakistan Electric Power Company
POL	Petrol, Oil, Lubricants
PSO	Pakistan State Oil
SBP	State Bank of Pakistan
SECP	Securities and Exchange Commission of Pakistan
SSGC	Sui Southern Gas Corporation
TFC	Term Finance Certificate
TPS	Transaction Processing System
WAPDA	Water and Power Development Authority
WAN	Wide Area Network

This casebook has been made possible by bringing together internationally published business cases written by the author. These cases were written to enable the management practices in Pakistani companies to be documented and used in the classroom so that students get to learn from and experience real world problems. By learning about the problems of real companies and the situations managers face during their day to day work through case studies, the knowledge imparted to university students and practising managers can be enhanced.

The seven cases in this casebook cover a variety of issues which fall under the ambit of corporate governance and management control. The cases on corporate governance relate to conditions under which governance breaks down and thus by analysing these, the analyst can try to define what is good corporate governance. Managers are often faced with situations that require anticipation and ability to guide their organization through major risks that may be faced. The cases include the actions of the board of directors, the role of the audit committee, the role of the corporate regulatory organization known as the Securities and Exchange Commission of Pakistan, and the interaction with the external auditors. A fact that differentiates the cases in this book from other casebooks is that in each case there are a number of issues relating to various areas of management of Pakistani companies. The cases challenge the analyst to identify different managerial aspects of the situations faced by companies and suggest solutions to the issues identified.

At the beginning of each case study, the case highlights and key points are mentioned as an introduction to the case. The Casebook on Corporate Governance and Management Practices in Pakistani Organizations can be used as a supplementary text for undergraduate, postgraduate, and executive courses that have an interest in teaching corporate governance by using case studies. All of the cases have been used in classrooms the world over and the author is grateful to each Pakistani company which allowed the case to be written.

All cases which were written after conducting interviews of company managers and examining corporate documentation have been officially allowed to be published by the companies concerned. Some cases were written from material in the public domain and as such do not contain any confidential information. However the author does not intend to illustrate either effective or ineffective handling of a managerial situation in any of the cases. The author may have disguised certain names and other identifying information in the case to protect confidentiality.

Muntazar Bashir Ahmed FCA
Lahore
15 July 2017

The focus of this book is on corporate governance and management practices which are dealt with via seven cases that the reader will find interesting as well as instructive. There are some common factors in the three cases related to corporate governance such as family members on the board, aggressive and unrealistic expectation of growth in profitability, and violation of business ethics. Two companies were so badly affected that they had to be liquidated while another suffered near bankruptcy and had to be bailed out by the foreign shareholders by injecting further capital.

The book can be used as a supplement to text books of management and should facilitate discussions in seminars and postgraduate courses. Each case study in this book introduces to the reader facts and real life situations where management of the company was required to take specific action. By analysing the management actions in class, students can discuss the pros and cons of the decisions taken and thus decide for themselves the appropriateness of actions taken.

The book does not present easy situations as the cases invariably bring together a variety of related situations requiring management decisions. By adopting an open approach to the issues, the reader will be able to decide on the resolution to management problems. Case studies help to bring the management decisions in the classroom but often there is no correct answer.

The book is structured as follows:

Section 1 deals briefly with the various thinking behind the codes of corporate governance in USA, UK, and Pakistan. This is followed by three case studies of Pakistani public limited companies and there are different issues dealing with the directors and other stakeholders.

Section 2 deals with a variety of management situations that most managers are likely to face. This is followed by four case studies again of Pakistani companies and each case has a specific issue that has to be addressed by the management.

For each case there are some assignment questions which are designed to facilitate a discussion rather than seeking a 'right answer'. In any management situation there is often incomplete information available yet managers have to decide and move ahead.

What is Corporate Governance?[1]

How is a corporation governed? Who has the authority to make decisions for a corporation and within what guidelines? These questions come under the ambit of corporate governance. In the United States, the governance of corporations is largely determined by state laws of incorporation. State laws typically say that each corporation must be 'managed by or under the direction of its boards of directors.' More specifically, corporate boards of directors are responsible for certain decisions on behalf of the corporation. At a minimum, as stated in most state statutes of incorporation, director approval is usually required for amending corporation bylaws, issuing shares, or declaring dividends. Also, the board alone can recommend that shareholders vote to amend articles of incorporation, dissolve the corporation, or sell the corporation. No other person or entity except the board can take these actions. That is why discussions of 'corporate governance' often focus on boards.

Overarching Principles[2]

The UK has identified the following five overarching principles and although generally derived from the UK Corporate Governance Code, they also underpin other countries' corporate governance codes. Most components of existing codes should relate to one or more of these principles. However, some of the principles go beyond the current scope of codes.

---

1   Source: http://www.corpgov.net/library/corporate-governance-defined/Accessed 12 May 2016.

2   Source: http://www.icaew.com/~/media/corporate/files/technical/corporate%20governance/dialogue%20in%20corporate%20governance/icaew%20tl%20q2%20web.ashx Accessed 12 May 2016.

Leadership

An effective board should head each company, steering the company to meet its business purpose in both the short and long term.

Capability

The board should have an appropriate mix of skills, experience, and independence to enable its members to discharge their duties and responsibilities effectively.

Accountability

The board should communicate to the company's shareholders and other stakeholders at regular intervals, a fair, balanced, and understandable assessment of how the company is achieving its business purpose and meeting its other responsibilities.

Sustainability

The board should guide the business to create value and allocate it fairly and sustainably to reinvestment and distributions to stakeholders, including shareholders, directors, employees, and customers.

Integrity

The board should lead the company to conduct its business in a fair and transparent manner that can withstand scrutiny by stakeholders.

THE CODE OF CORPORATE GOVERNANCE IN PAKISTAN[1]— BRIEF BACKGROUND

The investment decisions taken by the local and international investors are impacted by the governance practices. As markets compete to attract the capital from world over, companies are gauged by the investors using various factors that demonstrate sustainable track record. In order for Pakistani companies to compete globally, they have to follow enhanced corporate governance standards. This is a major factor towards making capital markets transparent, protecting rights of minority shareholders, and attracting and retaining foreign investment. The importance of corporate governance lies in its contribution both to business prosperity and to accountability.

The Securities and Exchange Commission of Pakistan (SECP) is the government agency tasked with the responsibility to raise the corporate governance standards in the country. In March 2002, the first effort was made when the Code of Corporate Governance (Code) was issued by SECP. This code was applicable to all public listed companies and was subsequently made part of the listing regulations of the three stock exchanges.[2] There have been revisions in the Code so that governance standards remain dynamic, relevant, and effective. This was also needed as the Pakistani corporate sector continues to develop. The objective was to further improve and raise the standards of corporate governance in the country while at the same time taking into consideration the global developments in corporate governance.

All Pakistani listed companies are required by the Securities and Exchange Commission of Pakistan to comply with the Code of Corporate Governance 2012. A Statement of Compliance with the code of corporate governance is required as part of the Annual Report containing the annual audited financial statements of listed companies and the auditors express their opinion on compliance with the code.

---

1   Source: http://jamapunji.pk/sites/default/files/CodeOfCorporateGovernance_2012_AmendedJuly2014.pdf Accessed on 1 October 2016.
2   The three exchanges were merged into one in 2016 and named as Pakistan Stock Exchange.

CASES IN CORPORATE GOVERNANCE

1.1 CALLMATE TELIPS (A) CHOICE OF ACCOUNTING POLICY

CASE HIGHLIGHTS AND KEY POINTS

Callmate Telips Telecom Limited (Callmate) was in the telecommunications business in which, during 2005, the regulatory controls were gradually being undone by the Government of Pakistan as part of an economic deregulation program. Callmate was the pioneer in the payphones and prepaid calling card industries in Pakistan and had significant opportunity to develop into a major business entity. The events in the case demonstrate that the company strategy as well as aggressive share price management could be dangerous if there are no checks on the directors. All the Directors of Callmate were close family members and the audit committee also consisted of three of the Directors.

The external audit firm for Callmate was A. F. Fergusons & Co (Ferguson) and they were an affiliate of Pricewaterhouse Coopers International. Fergusons was regarded among the top professional accounting firms in Pakistan. As Callmate was listed on the Karachi Stock Exchange, it was required to publish its financials quarterly after these had been reviewed by Fergusons. The company had received permission during early 1995 to enter into the Long Distance International market which was earlier the monopoly of the state firm Pakistan Telecommunications Company Limited (PTCL). A disagreement arose between the auditors of Callmate and the company directors on the accounting policy related to revenue recognition used in the financials of the half year ended December 2005. This dispute and the company trying to manage its share price led to a number of problems which became public knowledge as the company tried to malign the auditors.

The student, while going through this case, can examine the following:

1. The fundamental requirement by the capital markets worldwide that all corporate reports should include an independent opinion by a recognized audit firm. Recently, the bankruptcies in the corporate world (Enron, Parmalat, Bear Stearns, Barings, Societe Generale) raise doubts as to whether this is a realistic expectation. The move by the Securities and Exchange Commission in September 2008 to require US corporations to also adopt International Financial Reporting Standards (IFRS) is an important step towards comparability of results and hence improving corporate governance.

2. An obligation and degree of due care and transparency of the actions of the directors is required by all the stakeholders, especially the minority shareholders, in a public listed company. This can be discussed, as the case relates to a company where shares were closely held.

3. The audit committee should have primary responsibility for making a recommendation on the appointment, reappointment, and removal of external auditors. This recommendation should be made to the board. The audit committee should assess the qualification, expertise and resources, and effectiveness and independence of the external auditors annually.

4. The accounting policies adopted to prepare financial statements should not only be

consistent, but must take into account the substance of the transaction and not just its legal form. Simply to follow last year's accounting policy is not a reliable basis if the business nature has changed. It is however debatable whether all audit firms can influence their clients to use appropriate policies. They normally risk losing the audit assignment and a lot of fees.

5. The impact of the threat of removal of the auditor by the directors on the quality of the audit opinion can be discussed. As various large corporate failures have shown, the traditional statutory audit has rarely raised any red flags in time to prevent a collapse.

6. The efficacy of the regulatory regime of the audit firms and of the public listed companies could be analyzed. In Pakistan and in most countries worldwide, the professional audit firms were and in some countries still are self-regulated. The failure of Arthur Anderson in the United States caused a major upheaval in the public accounting firms' regulatory and operating structures. There was an immediate separation of the pure audit work, also known as compliance, and management consulting services. These two are now being done by separate independent firms.

7. There is a reference to a type of financing for short-selling called 'badla' and the fact that a very large number of shares of the company were being traded through this highly speculative process showed that the ethical values of the management were not of a high standard.

POTENTIAL USES OF THE CASE

1. This case can be used in an MBA/executive program to highlight the precarious position of the external auditor within the framework of corporate governance. The power of the directors, in a company whose shares are closely held, can be so overbearing that the independent opinion on the financial statements rarely provides the intended assurance to the stakeholders.

2. It can also be used in a class on business ethics, as the board of directors (BOD) was very aggressive and went along with the auditors until there were differences of

opinion. Its reaction in the form of accusations and statements showed that it was determined to have its way and at all stages was very conscious of the share price.

While management must be sensitive to company share price, the 'tail should not wag the dog,' i.e. the market price should reflect a true value of the company's business. It is the duty of management to enhance shareholder value by good decisions and not by releasing selective information to manipulate the market price.

The SECP had also written to the company to provide the details that it had withheld from the auditors. In short, the management was manipulating the KSE share price through financial disclosures such as inflated profits and bonus shares, as well as providing incomplete and incorrect information to the SECP. The five-year share price graph shows that the share price was very volatile and always fluctuating in a band.

The core financial issue is the policy adopted for recognition of revenue. The extracts of financial statements are included to help in quantifying the financial impact of using each of the two accounting policies to recognize revenue on the sale in December 2005 of cards for export:

1. Dispatch of cards method—done by the company; and

2. Consumption of cards method—calculation (estimation) required.

The summary of financial results shows how the receivables increased from Rs. 709 million in 30 June 2005 to Rs. 1.6 billion as at 31 December 2005, as a consequence of the policy adopted. The rupees 907 million can be deduced to have been substantially related to the cards dispatched in December.

With respect to organizational issues, the company's directors were aggressive as the business growth was very rapid and they were not in any mood to accept anything that could jeopardize the rise of the share price. The shares on floatation in mid-2004 had a price of Rs. 15.25 and reached Rs. 83.15 during December 2006. Since the shares were closely held—as can be deduced from the ease with which the dissenting auditor A. F. Ferguson & Co, Chartered Accountants (Ferguson) was removed—the Directors wanted no constraints.

ASSIGNMENT QUESTIONS

1. What was the cause of the breakdown in the relations of the company with its auditor? Do you think the auditors were correct in their point of view?

2. Describe the various laws and regulations that apply to published financial statements in Pakistan.

3. Do you suggest any changes in the regulation? How would they impact this case?

4. Do you agree with the various accusations that the management of the company made against the auditors?

5. Do the regulations governing the corporate sector ensure that the auditors' opinion is totally independent and unbiased? Do you agree that Ferguson should have been replaced? Explain your answer.

The case examines corporate governance of the company by examining the role of the external auditor, the conduct of the Board of Directors, and the regulator of public listed companies, the Securities and Exchange Commission of Pakistan (SECP). There were a series of events which caused a profitable company to rapidly became a pariah on the Stock Exchange and was ultimately suspended from the bourse.

CASE TEXT: CALLMATE TELIPS (A) CHOICE OF ACCOUNTING POLICY[1]

A young business graduate was an investor in equity shares on the Karachi Stock Exchange (KSE). He was evaluating how his portfolio of investments had performed during the calendar year 2006. On 15 December 2006, he read in the local newspaper that the Security and Exchange Commission of Pakistan (SECP) had issued a directive to all three stock exchanges of the country to suspend trading of Callmate Telips Telecom Limited (Callmate)

---

1   This case has been written on the basis of published sources only. Consequently, the interpretation and perspectives presented in the case are not necessarily those of Callmate Telips Telecom Limited or any of its employees.

shares for 60 days. He owned a significant number of shares in that company. During the past few months the company name had been in the press and under discussion all around the KSE. This was after it had disagreed on the revenue recognition policy with its auditors, A. F. Ferguson & Co., Chartered Accountants (Ferguson), and accused them of causing the fall in the Callmate share price on the KSE. The graduate was aware that Ferguson was a reputable audit firm and was associated with Pricewaterhouse Coopers (PWC), the largest of the big four international public accounting firms.

The young graduate had taken a course in his studies which mentioned that the role of the external auditor was to give an independent opinion on financial statements and that this was very important for a healthy securities market. He was uncertain as to how this was ensured, as it appeared that Ferguson had been replaced on 12 October 2006, by Callmate simply by holding an extraordinary general meeting where the shareholders voted against the incumbent audit firm. The graduate had also suffered a major loss on his shares in Callmate so he decided to look into what had led the SECP to suspend the trading of the shares.

Corporate Profile

Callmate was a Pakistan-based public limited company listed at the KSE and was operating in the payphones and the prepaid calling card business all over Pakistan. The company was formed subsequent to the merger between CallTel (Private) Limited and Telefon International Project Services (Private) Limited on 11 November 2003.

The annual report of Callmate for 2005 provided the details of the background of the company. It stated that CallTel (Private) Limited had been incorporated as a private company in May 1999 and had principally engaged in providing prepaid calling card services in Pakistan. The company signed a novation agreement with the government-owned Pakistan national operator, Pakistan Telecommunication Corporation Limited (PTCL) to set up, operate, and maintain a prepaid calling card service for a period of five years, on the company's behalf, commencing from August 1999 under the brand name 'Callmate'. However, in 2002 the company entered into a new agreement, which abrogated the earlier agreement and this agreement was also for five years starting on March 2002.

Telefone International Project Services (Private) Limited (Telips) was incorporated in 1991. Telips had obtained a license from the government of Pakistan to install, own, and operate a network of card-operated wire line payphones throughout the country. It had embarked to set up the required nationwide payphones network all across Pakistan. In November 2003, the scheme of arrangement to amalgamate CallTel (Private) Limited with Telips, effective 31 December 2002, was approved by the High Court in the province of Sindh. Consequently, all the properties, assets, rights, liabilities, obligations, and reserves were transferred to the new vested company called Callmate Telips Telecom (Pvt) Limited (Callmate). Callmate was converted to a public listed company in December 2003 and was listed on the KSE on 1 June 2004.

As a result of the deregulation of the telecom industry in Pakistan, Callmate became the first long distance and international (LDI[2]) operator in Pakistan's history, enabling it to terminate and originate traffic for long distance with the new cost-effective LDI platform. The formal award of the license took place on 12 July 2004, when the company was issued the first-ever LDI license, thus bringing an end to the telecom monopoly in Pakistan.

Business of the Company

Callmate envisioned itself as a leading telecommunication operator in Pakistan by continuing its prominent contribution to the growth and development of the industry and providing quality services throughout the country. In parallel to its diverse expansion plans, the company intended to provide a full range of efficient telecommunication services and high-quality customer support and maintenance services in order to achieve the highest possible functional status. The board of directors of the company consisted of the following (mainly family members whose shareholding was as follows):

Name	Title	Percentage of shares held
1. Ahmed Jamil Ansari	Chairman	23
2. Mohammad Ajmal Ansari	Chief Executive Officer	4

---

2   LDI stands for Long Distance and International and is the name commonly given to the process of allowing private carriers to compete with the incumbent national telecom operator. Most countries are now opening up their telecom markets for private carriers and allowing more carriers to compete with each other. LDI traffic has two parts: national long distance and international long distance.

3. Hasan Jamil Ansari	Executive Director	6
4. Yuba Jamil Ansari	Non-Executive Director	3
5. Maria Jamil Ansari	Non-Executive Director	negligible
6. Abu Shamim M. Ariff	Non-Executive Director	negligible
7. Nuzhat Ikramullah	Non-Executive Director	negligible

The audit committee consisted of the chairman, chief executive officer, and the executive director and it held three meetings during 2005.

The company's strategy was directed towards furnishing telecommunication services to meet the needs of the market. Due to the low rate of penetration, there was considerable scope for expansion. Callmate was positioned to emerge as a key player in a deregulated telecommunications sector due to the extensive infrastructure for payphones and distribution network for calling card services which had a brand identity. Callmate intended to take advantage of the deregulated telecommunication opportunities in the country by applying for various possible telecom licenses including LDI and Wireless Local Loop (WLL) to enable it to provide cheaper and cost-effective communication facilities to its customers. The company thus experienced good growth; its sales increased from Rs. 1.335 billion in 2004 to Rs. 4.161 billion in 2006 (Rs. 60=US$1), while profits rose from Rs. 67 million in 2004 to Rs. 603 million in 2006 (see Exhibit 1).

Auditor Reports

The publication of quarterly financial statements by public listed companies was required by the Companies Ordinance 1984 and the Securities and Exchange Ordinance 1969. The SECP was responsible for ensuring compliance with regulations by the listed companies. The Institute of Chartered Accountants of Pakistan (ICAP) was the regulating body of all audit firms; it was a statutory body formed under the Chartered Accountants Ordinance 1961. The ICAP had implemented a mandatory Quality Control Review Program since 1999 that required all firms to undergo a review of the working papers. Any firm that did not receive a satisfactory rating was not qualified to be appointed as auditor of a listed company. Among other guidelines, the audit firms were required to conduct their reviews and audits in accordance with the International Auditing Standards (IAS). This required that the financial statements being audited were prepared on the principles espoused by the IAS.

All financial reporting formats were according to the International Financial Reporting Standards (IFRS)[3], which provided guidance on presentation and disclosure. The other factors impacting financial reporting in Pakistan were the local statutory requirements such as:

- The Companies' Ordinance 1984

- Directives of the regulatory bodies such as the SECP

- Industry-specific legislation

- Generally accepted accounting principles

In accordance with the rules, the management of Callmate was required to release quarterly financial statements for publication after the external audit firm had reviewed those statements. A review was different from the annual audit, as its scope was very limited; this was stated in the auditor's report included as part of the published financial statements. After such a review of the half yearly statements of the company, as of 31 December 2005, the audit staff of Ferguson disagreed with the accounting policy used for recognizing revenue related to LDI calling cards. Accordingly, the staff mentioned in its report (see Exhibit 2) that the profit was overstated in the financial statements by Rs. 280 million.

The financial statements prepared by the Callmate management for the half year to 31 December 2005 were based on the accounting policies which were unchanged from the previous year (see Exhibits 3 and 4). The company had recently been allowed to sell prepaid calling services from overseas and it had shipped a large quantity of cards, all of which were shown as part of revenues. The auditors felt that these cards needed to be shown as unrealized sales, as the services were yet to be provided.

The company felt that if the revenue recognition policy was changed, the revenue in the fourth quarter would also suffer a setback. The reason was that if revenue was recognized when the cards were actually utilized by the customers (usage-based policy), rather than at the time of sale to dealers (dispatch-based policy), this would defer revenues to later

---

3   The Securities and Exchange Commission in the United States had recently introduced a gradual plan for US public companies to use the IFRS as the future basis for reporting in the United States.

periods. The only consequence of this change would have been a lag of almost a quarter in the sales revenue being recorded. And due to this shift taking place in the fourth quarter for the year ended 30 June 2006 (as reported in the company's report for the quarter ending March 2006), profitability would have shown a one-time dip and normalized thereafter.

Removal of Auditors

A rift had begun to emerge between the company and its external auditors, Ferguson, when, according to the company, the auditors declined to agree with the revenue recognition policy which recognized the revenues on the basis of the sale of cards, without having to wait for usage of these cards. It was a common practice worldwide and in Pakistan that the revenues were booked on the basis of sale of prepaid cards and not on their usage, as according to a survey, 25 per cent of the prepaid cards were never used. Ferguson had earlier been allowing the company to book its revenues on the basis of sale of cards and not usage for four years since 2001. Callmate management felt the auditors had changed their view even though they had given a clean audit report for the year ended June 2005.

Callmate was an important and large client of Ferguson and the accounts for the year ended 30 June 2005 (see Exhibit 5) showed that a substantial fee was paid by the company. As the allegations by the company were getting serious, Ferguson's management in a letter to the SECP stated that the disagreement was not over the revenue recognition policy, but some other facts that had been requested from the company which were not being provided to them. Hence, there was an inevitable delay in approving the company accounts for the year ended 30 June 2006.

The company also claimed that Ferguson failed to meet all timelines for deliverables agreed upon between the company and it. According to the agreement, Ferguson had to deliver the company's initialed accounts for the year ended 30 June 2006, with the audit clearance letter by 28 August 2006; this time limit was not met. Later, in a meeting with the company, the auditors committed to deliver the accounts by September 4 and on that basis the company announced the holding of its board meeting for 12 September and circulated the notice in the KSE. As no accounts initialed by Ferguson were available for the board meeting held on 12 September, the company was only able to forward management accounts which had not been reviewed by the auditors to KSE. This, the company felt, had thrown the shareholders into confusion as to exactly what was going on and had affected the share price (see Exhibit 6).

A notice sent by the company to Ferguson claimed that by making the policy change without any prior notice to the company management the auditors had acted improperly. The actual notice read: 'But, A. F. Ferguson, acting completely unprofessionally disregarded company's repute and the interest of shareholders.' It then went on to say, 'This practice of A. F. Ferguson has severely damaged Callmate and its scrip repute in the stock market and the company has sustained huge losses.' Sources inside the company also remarked: 'We suspect that the external auditors have been involved in share trading, or something.[4]

Another notice issued by the company said, 'As a result of non-submission of audited financial statements by the auditor of the company A. F. Ferguson & Co Chartered Accountants and the fact that despite making all the efforts to resolve the difference pertaining to the revenue recognition policy, the Company has no option other than to seek removal of the auditors through a special resolution to be passed at an extraordinary general meeting of shareholders.'[5]

On 20 September, the company issued a notice to the shareholders calling for an extraordinary general meeting on 12 October. The principal item on the agenda was the change of auditors, from the present auditor group to one of the three that the company proposed. The right of appointment of auditors was statutorily that of the shareholders and as a large proportion of the equity was generally held by the management, any resolutions moved in almost all listed company cases were certain to be passed. It was, however, unclear whether the regulator, SECP, would step in to overturn the shareholders' decision. The pattern of shares held in Callmate was as follows:

Board of directors and family members	36 per cent
Financial institutions	19 per cent
General public (traded on KSE)	36 per cent
Foreign and others	9 per cent

---

4   With permission from Business Recorder, 18 September 2006.
5   Ibid.

On 20 September, Ferguson also sent a letter to SECP which contradicted the company's resolution for the extraordinary general meeting (EGM). The auditors claimed that the disagreement stated in the notice sent to the shareholders was incorrect and that the real reason was other important information that they had sought from the company but had not been received up to 14 September 2006. As a result, on 25 September 2006, the SECP issued a letter pointing out, among other items, that in its opinion the notice of the EGM was not in accordance with the law and that provision existed in the law that if an auditor was removed by a company, the SECP could appoint a new auditor. For an extreme case of fraud, the National Accountability Ordinance, 1999 (see Exhibit 7), had introduced stiffer penalties that were applicable to company management as well.

The company, after consulting its lawyers, went ahead with the EGM and also filed a constitutional petition to challenge the directives of the SECP that only the commission had authority to appoint a new auditor in place of the former auditor removed by the company. In the EGM held on 12 October 2006, the company successfully removed Ferguson as external auditors, claiming professional negligence that resulted in huge losses to the company shareholders. Later, on 8 December 2006, a judge of the Lahore High Court, Rawalpindi Bench, issued an order that restrained the SECP from appointing the auditor for Callmate in response to a writ petition filed by Barrister Aitzaz Ahsan.

A legal notice was also served to Ferguson by the management in which it was claimed that as a direct consequence of Ferguson's negligence and deliberate breach of obligations, the market capitalization had deteriorated by more than 50 per cent, despite the company's profitability and operations remaining stable. Also, the company's plan to have its scrip listed in Dubai had to be aborted and its share had taken a more than 50 per cent fall, with the scrip's reputation having become the joke of the stock market.

On 11 October 2006, Callmate announced that it had given a mandate to Orix Investment Bank Pakistan Limited (OIBPL) as its financial advisor to arrange a 'badla'[6] financing

---

6   'Badla' is essentially a facility for financing share purchases extended by brokerages and banks that allows buyers to obtain highly leveraged positions in the market. A brokerage client can delay the payment for purchases indefinitely by paying badla overnight finance rates via an overnight sale and buy-back mechanism. The extent of leverage through such non-bank financing for COT (Carry Over Transactions, another name for badla) is not transparent and underlying security transactions are typically speculative. A feature of this short-term finance provision is that a large proportion of funding comes from insurance and mutual funds. This accentuates the risk for both investors and users of badla financing. In addition, badla also creates scope for market manipulation and increases systemic risk.
Investor: Badla investor wishes to lend money to buy overnight shares at a price that should give a return about four to five

transaction of Rs. 750 million for Callmate shares. Badla is a means of financing which exacerbates speculative activity in Pakistan's markets. Badla financing had reached an amount of more than Rs. 35 billion and the badla rate generally ranged between 10 and 18 per cent.

According to the mandate, OIBPL would advise and assist Callmate in the designing, structuring, and undertaking of book-building exercises and the placement of a large block of common equity shares for Callmate accumulating to Rs. 750 million. OIBPL would also act as the placement agent and book-building agent for the entire badla financing on behalf of Callmate and diversify the distribution of offerings that included retail and the institutional investor's base.

The financial advisor of Callmate, if appropriate and if so required, would also undertake designing, distributing, and structuring badla financing for Callmate, with premium over par value. Further, he would test the market to determine the expected badla financing cost for the purchase of Callmate shares under the prevailing stock market scenario. OIBPL had executed the transaction and Callmate had agreed to pay 1.5 per cent of Rs. 750 million as the advisory fee to the financial advisor. OIBPL was also in the maturity stage to finalize a deal with a Middle Eastern group to be the strategic partner of Callmate.

Callmate, a leading long distance and international (LDI) private operator in Pakistan, which intended reaching out to the United States, the United Kingdom, and Canada, was set to begin its operations in Europe soon. The company had depicted a growth in all key indicators over the past five years. Its revenue increased at a five-year combined annual growth rate (CAGR) of 62 per cent to Rs. 3.04 billion in FY05, from Rs. 273 million in FY00 and gross profits surged at a CAGR of 84 per cent.

The company also turned a profit of Rs. 432 million for FY05, from a loss of Rs. 30 million in FY00. Profitability of the company during the first nine months of the fiscal year ending 30 June 2006, rose by 230 per cent to Rs. 716 million (see Exhibit 1), translating in diluted earning per shares (EPS) of Rs. 10.95.

---

per cent above short-term rates. At the same time as the buy, they execute a next-day sell contract for the same parcel. Speculator: Market holder cannot fund a shareholding so they overnight sell to a badla investor at a cost of carry four to five per cent above short-term rates. At the same time, they execute a next-day buy contract for the same parcel of shares.

Even though the profitability and the operations of the company appeared to be intact, the shareholders in Callmate had suffered an estimated loss of Rs. 4 billion, as the stock price of the company dipped by an incredible 56 per cent in seven months, from Rs. 108 to Rs. 47. At the heart of the problem was the dispute between Callmate and the external auditors, Ferguson.

A newspaper report on 8 November 2006 said that the ICAP had referred Ferguson to its investigation committee to see if the firm had engaged in professional misconduct. The investigation committee would begin its deliberation on 8 November. While Ferguson had been facing various allegations of professional misconduct for the last many months, this was the first time in its history that it would have to face formal investigation for professional misconduct in Pakistan.

The ICAP had taken this step on the complaint of Nadeem Ahmed, advocate of Ahmed and Qazi Associates.

> Under Section 20-H of the Chartered Accountants Ordinance 1961 (X of 1961), when conducting 'inquiry' into professional misconduct of A. F. Ferguson, the Investigation Committee shall be deemed to be a civil court and shall have the same powers as are vested in a civil court under Code of Civil Procedure 1908, specially in relation to summoning and enforcing the attendance of any person and examining him on oath, the discovery and production of any document and receiving evidence on affidavit.[7]

Chartered Accountants Ordinance 1961 (X of 1961) gave the Investigation Committee the powers, whenever allegations of professional misconduct were proven in its inquiry, to remove the firm from the membership of ICAP for a period of five years. However, given the seriousness of allegations of the case, the investigation committee could even decide to refer the misconduct to the High Court of Sindh, in which case, if the case against it proved, there could even be a permanent ban on operating in Pakistan. Ahmed told *Business Recorder* that he was also keeping partners of PWC in London fully informed.

According to him, the shareholders' complaint against Ferguson's misconduct should be

---

7   'Ferguson/PWC may face ban on practice,' with permission from <u>Business Recorder</u>, 8 November 2006.

seen as a class action, an attempt to seek justice in the form of cancellation of the PWC/ Ferguson license to practice in Pakistan.

The SECP and the company had long been in disagreement over appointment of auditors. The regulator had also expressed doubt that the company was not providing exact figures of its profit and bonus. The SECP asked the company to accept the officially-nominated auditors, but the company refused the condition. This led to a severe controversy between the company and the regulator and resulted in the ban for 60 days on company's shares trading in the three stock exchanges on 9 December 2006. This action was taken by SECP after it had received news that the company management had traded 36.4 million shares out of the total number of 65.6 million shares, about 51 per cent of the total number of shares issued.

The SECP notification said: 'Callmate had declared a bonus issue without compliance with the provisions of Rule 6 of the Companies (issue of capital) Rules, 1996' and the notification added, 'Upon an examination of our record, we concur that the Company has failed to comply with the said Rule 6 and has failed to provide a satisfactory explanation in this regard as sought by the Commission via its letter dated 4 December 2006 and 5 December 2006 addressed to the Company.' The notification further said, 'In view of the aforesaid, the declaration of bonus issue is prime facie contrary to the law, and the Commission is taking necessary steps to proceed against the Company for acting in violation of Rules.' It said, 'In these circumstance, the Commission is satisfied that it is in the public interest to suspend the trading of the shares of the Company in order to avoid a negative impact on the interest of shareholders due to the effect these development are likely to have on the trading value of the shares.'

On Friday, 8 December, the Callmate share price hit its lower circuit breaker, after upper circuit breakers had been witnessed for the last four or five consecutive days at the KSE. On that Friday, the scrip had opened at Rs. 87.50 and closed at Rs. 83.15, shedding Rs. 4.35 (circuit breaker came into effect if a share price fell more than five per cent in one trading session at the KSE).

Experts believed that suspension of trading in Callmate shares was the right step by the SECP, as the scrip might have witnessed further lower circuit breakers in the sessions to be held. Lower circuits could have pushed the market index below the 10,000-points level, they calculated, as a large number of scrips of Callmate were traded through badla or continuous funding system (CFS) in the market. According to the sources, the decision had been taken following the information that the company had sold around 36.4 million shares in the market out of a total of 65.6 million shares.

CONCLUSION

A journalist of a leading newspaper opined: 'Whether it was the "revenue recognition policy" relating to the pre-paid calling card services or "certain other pending matters" that soured the relationship between Callmate Telips Telecom Limited and its auditor A. F. Ferguson & Co., the matter came in full view as both parties began washing dirty linen in public. It would be impossible to do full justice to reproduce the contentions of the two parties in this space, but suffice it to say that the auditors insisted on issuing a "qualified" audit report and the company management insisted on accepting nothing but a "clean" one. As angry letters were thrown at each other with the stock exchange as the middleman, the action was said to have followed after "all efforts to resolve the differences had failed."'

But the corporate and accounting communities were surprised that a high-profile company and the top-notch audit firm of the country should have opted to pull punches in public. That was what made Callmate a case of great corporate interest. It was difficult to draw a parallel of such mudslinging between a client and its auditor. Qualified audit reports were routinely issued by auditors, to which managements may or may not have agreed, but all of that passed off in mostly a peaceful and quiet manner. The full-blown case of Callmate appeared, to many professional people, to be less as standing up for the right and more a matter of personal pride.

At the end of each calendar year, the young business graduate reviewed the performance of his equity portfolio so as to decide what changes he needed to make in his investment strategy. The year 2006 had been full of news about Callmate, so he decided to revisit the various facts reported by the media to better understand what had happened.

EXHIBIT 1

SUMMARY OF FINANCIAL STATISTICS

The following chart shows the key statistics as at each quarterly reporting date between 30 June 2005 and 30 June 2006:

	RUPEES IN MILLIONS			RS. 60=US$1 DOLLAR		
Balance Sheet	As at 30 June 2006	As at 31 Mar 2006	As at 31 Dec 2005	As at 30 Sept 2005	As at 30 June 2005	As at 30 June 2004
Total Assets	3,318.0	3,039.7	3,197.3	2,151.0	2,139.0	867.5
Trade Debts	994.4	989.2	1,613.5		709.1	164.5
Shareholders' Equity	1,437.6	1,615.2	1,391.7	1,121.4	949.7	517.4

	RUPEES IN MILLIONS			RS. 60=US$1 DOLLAR		
Profit & Loss Account	For the Year Ended June 2006	For the 3rd Qtr. Ended Mar 2006	For the 2nd Qtr. Ended Dec 2005	For the 1st Qtr. Ended Sept 2005	For the Year Ended June 2005	For the Year Ended June 2004
Sales and Services–Net	4,161.4	943.0	1,456.2	957.9	3,040.4	1336.0
Net Profit (Before Tax)	636.7	241.8	305.8	340.0	673.1	114.6
Net Profit (After Tax)	603.5	223.5	2703	222.0	432.3	67.7
EPS (Rs. per share)	9.23	3.76	8.28	4.42	8.60	2.5
Reserves Used to Issue Bonus Shares (Rs. in millions)	50.25					
Share price–HIGH	Rs. 113.00	Rs. 79.65	Rs. 56.40	Rs. 37.50	Rs. 17.05	Rs. 10.00
LOW	Rs. 52.05	Rs. 97.05	Rs. 79.65	Rs. 56.40	Rs. 37.50	Rs. 17.05

Source: Company financial reports.

EXHIBIT 2

CASES IN CORPORATE GOVERNANCE   19

AUDIT REVIEW REPORT ON THE HALF YEARLY FINANCIAL STATEMENTS AS AT 31 DECEMBER 2005

Review report to the members

1. We have reviewed the annexed balance sheet of Callmate Telips Telecom Limited as at 31 December 2005, and the related profit and loss account, cash flow statement, and statement of changes in equity together with the notes forming part thereof (here-in-after referred to as the 'financial statements'), for the half-year then ended. These financial statements are the responsibility of the Company's management. Our responsibility is to issue a report on these financial statements based on our review. The figures of the profit and loss account for the quarters ended 31 December 2004 and 2005 have not been reviewed as we are required to review only the cumulative figures for the half year ended 31 December 2005.

2. We conducted our review in accordance with the International Standard on Review Engagements 2400. This standard requires that we plan and perform the review to obtain moderate assurance as to whether the financial statements are free of material missstatement. A review is limited primarily to inquiries of Company's personnel and analytical procedures applied to financial data and thus provides less assurance than an audit. We have not performed an audit and, accordingly, we do not express as audit opinion.

3. As more fully explained in note 3.2, the Company has recognised the total revenue on export of international prepaid calling cards amounting to Rs. 476.006 million as earned though these cards were unactivated and unutilized as at 31 December 2005. Further, the Company has continued to recognise as revenue the unutilized balance of local prepaid calling cards which as per computerized report amounted to Rs. 135.130 million as at 31 December 2005. As no services have been rendered by the Company, the aforementioned unutilized balance of Rs. 611.136 million, inclusive of export sales, in accordance with the International Accounting Standard 18—Revenue, should have been accounted for as unearned and reflected as such in the balance sheet. Instead, the Company has preferred to continue with the past practice of accruing thereagainst the cost component (calling charges) which

EXHIBIT 2 (CONTINUED)

amounted to Rs. 275.778 million, inclusive of Rs. 228.483 million on export sales on estimated basis. This has resulted in an overstatement of profit after taxation for the half year ended 31 December 2005 by Rs. 280.265 million.

4.   Based on our review, except for the effects of the matter reported in paragraph 3 above, nothing has come to our attention that causes us to believe that the annexed financial statements are not presented fairly, in all material respects, in accordance with approved accounting standards as applicable in Pakistan.

5.   Without qualifying our review report, we draw attention to the following matters:

(i)   The Company, as more fully explained in note 11.1, has disputed Pakistan Telecommunication Company Limited (PTCL) charges amounting to Rs. 246 million billed for unsuccessful calls and as such has not made any provision thereagainst.

(ii)   The Company has not recognised PTCL charges for the period March 2001 to June 2004 and the additional tax liability on withholding tax, as explained in notes 11.2 and 11.3 respectively; and

(iii) Lawsuit, as discussed in note 8, filed by the Company during the year ended 20 June 2004 in the

Source: Company periodic report.

EXHIBIT 3

CASES IN CORPORATE GOVERNANCE   21

EXTRACTS FROM DIRECTORS REVIEW
FOR HALF YEAR ENDED ON 31 DECEMBER 2005

Directors' Review

Dear Shareholders,
The Board of Directors of Callmate Telips Telecom Limited feel great pleasure to present the un-audited financial statements of your company, reviewed by the auditors, for the half-year ended on 31 December 2005.

Financial Overview

Complete results of the company for the half year are fully disclosed in the financial statements accompanying this report, however salient features of the results for the half year are as follows:

	For the half year ended	
	31 December 2005	31 December 2004
	... Rupees in '000 ...	
Sales and services—net	2,414,060	995,834
Gross profit	868,036	237,418
Earning before interest and tax (EBIT)	666,351	105,460
Financial charges	20,521	6,429
Net profit before taxation	645,830	99,031
Net profit after taxation	492,251	63,706
Earning per share (Rupees)	8.28	1.07

Rs. in '000

Your Directors are pleased to propose appropriation of profit as follows:

Profit available for appropriation	797,478
Appropriations	
Transfer to reserve for issuance of 10 per cent second interim bonus shares	59,424
	738,054

The board is pleased to state that despite increasing pressure of competitive business environment, your company managed to achieve an enormous growth, posting an increase in net sales by 142 per cent as compared with the same period last year (SPLY). Gross Profit also improved to 36 per cent from 24 per cent in SPLY. Net profit after taxation showed a remarkable improvement of 6.73 times as compared to SPLY which registered an increment of Rs. 7.21 in Earnings per Share (EPS) leading to Rs. 8.28. Our remarkable results are mainly due to the aggressive customer offerings and launch of new business segments.

Your company has launched International Calling Card with the unique concept in prepaid calling cards by offering dual connectivity (on a single calling card) to different market segments across the globe. We have received an admirable response from the market which has encouraged us to make more efforts in this segment. In the first phase of operations, we have launched this dual connectivity card in North America and United Kingdom, which in second phase will be extended to other countries. The initial focus would be Pakistani segment of population living in those territories and thereafter focus would be made towards Chinese, Indian and Bangladeshi segments. Your company capitalized on the opportunities created and successfully carved out its share.

The management of your company is also well cognizant of the International Accounting Standards on revenue recognition even more now on account of launching of international calling cards and has preferred to review it in detail at year end, rather than at mid-term.

Dividend

Considering the noteworthy performance of your company during the first six months, the Board is pleased to announce second interim bonus issue of 10 per cent (10 shares for every 100 shares held) leading total payout for the half year to 17.5 per cent.

Future Outlook

Your company is always dedicated to invest in new technologies and ventures for ultimate increase in shareholders value, Local Loop (LL) is just one of the new ventures which will be launched very soon and we believe that this will also add to the shareholders value.

EXHIBIT 3 (CONTINUED)

CASES IN CORPORATE GOVERNANCE   23

Your management is currently exploring the possibility of offshore listing at Dubai. Our initiative of offshore listing and raising equity finance is consistent with our plans to expand into other lines of telecommunication business in Pakistan and also further consolidate business interests abroad. We are currently in the process of exploring the possibility of offshore listing with investment advisors of repute.

Contingencies

As disclosed in the note 11 to the financial statements, your management has taken those matters with concerned parties aggressively and is very confident that the final outcome will be in the Company's favour.

Strategy

Your company has reaped the benefits of sales driven strategy to achieve targets and to capture more market share in the second quarter ended on 31 December 2005 and relaxed credit terms due to which trade debts were increased which have been substantially recovered subsequently, as disclosed in note 5.1 to the annexed financial statements.

Vote of Thanks

Source: Company periodic report.

EXTRACTS FROM NOTES TO THE FINANCIAL STATEMENTS (UNAUDITED) FOR THE HALF YEAR ENDED 31 DECEMBER 2005

1. Legal status and operations

Callmate Telips Telecom Limited is a public company incorporated in Pakistan under the Companies Ordinance, 1984, and its shares are listed on the Karachi Stock Exchange. The registered office of the Company is situated at 99-CF, 1/5, Clifton, Karachi.

The Company is principally engaged in providing calling card services and operates a network of card operated wire line pay phones in Pakistan.

Effective from 12 July 2004, the Pakistan Telecommunication Authority (PTA) has awarded the Long Distance International (LDI) License to the Company which shall be valid for a term of 20 years. The commercial operations of LDI business commenced from 1 January 2005.

The Company is evaluating the option for listing its securities on the Dubai International Financial Exchange.

2. Basis for Preparation

These financial statements are unaudited and are being submitted to shareholders in accordance with Section 245 of the Companies Ordinance, 1984 and International Accounting Standard (IAS) 34—'Interim Financial Reporting'. The figures for the half year ended 31 December 2005 have, however, been subjected to limited scope review by the auditors as required by the Code of Corporate Governance.

EXHIBIT 4 (CONTINUED)

CASES IN CORPORATE GOVERNANCE   25

3. Accounting policies

3.1 The accounting policies adopted in the preparation of these half yearly financial statements are the same as those applied in the preparation of the audited published financial statements of the company for the year ended 30 June 2005.

3.2 Export sale

During December 2005, the Company has launched international prepaid calling cards which can be used in other countries for origination/termination of calls from/to Pakistan. Accordingly, an agreement has been signed with a distributor based in USA for the distribution of cards in UK, USA and Canada. The first shipment of such cards was made on 30 December 2005 amounting to Rs. 476.006 million which were activated subsequent to 31 December 2005.

The company has adopted the same accounting policy in respect of the export sale as is followed for local sales i.e. on dispatch/delivery to distributors/dealers with the exception that unactivated cards exported are also recognised as sale. Accordingly, the company in respect of the aforementioned shipment has recognised the total amount of Rs. 476.006 million, included in sales, as earned during the current period on the contention that the risks and rewards associated with cards have been transferred and accrued on estimation the cost component (calling charges) thereagainst amounting to Rs. 228.483 million in these financial statements.

Source: Company report for the half year ended 31 December 2005.

EXTRACTS FROM NOTES TO THE FINANCIAL STATEMENTS FOR THE YEAR ENDED 30 JUNE 2005

	2005 Rupees	2004 Rupees
24.2 Auditors' remuneration		
Audit fee	900,000	750,000
Special audit, certification and reportings	–	500,000
Fee for review of half yearly accounts	375,000	
Out of pocket expenses	137,713	84,850
	1,412,713	1,334,850

Source: Company Annual Report.

EXHIBIT 6

CASES IN CORPORATE GOVERNANCE   27

2006 KSE PRICE CHART

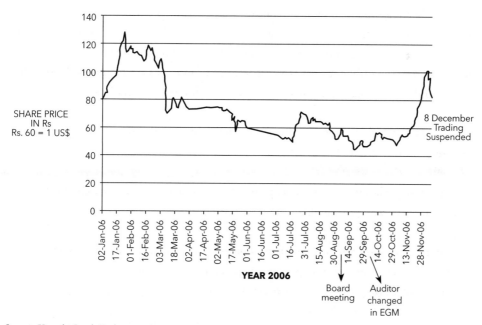

SHARE PRICE
IN Rs
Rs. 60 = 1 US$

YEAR 2006

8 December
Trading
Suspended

Board
meeting

Auditor
changed
in EGM

Source: Karachi Stock Exchange prices.

EXHIBIT 7

ACCOUNTABILITY ORDINANCE[8]

The National Accountability Ordinance, 1999 (the 'Ordinance of 1999') was introduced to, among other reasons, eradicate corruption and corrupt practices in Pakistan. Upon promulgation, the Ordinance of 1999 was initially pressed into service to prosecute the holders of public office against misappropriation of public money. While retaining the focus on preservation of the public money, the Ordinance of 1999 has been amended from time to time not only for legislative improvements but also for expansion of its scope.

Section 9 of the Ordinance of 1999 defines the offence of corruption and corrupt practices, which definition includes the following:

> A holder of public office, or any other person, is said to commit or to have committed the offense of corruption and corruption practices:
> [...]
> if he dishonestly or fraudulently misappropriates or otherwise converts for his own use, or for the use of any other person, any property entrusted to him, or under his control, or willfully allows any other person to do so.

The Ordinance of 1999 defines the expression 'person,' as used in Section 9, to include:

> ... In the case of a company or a body corporate, the sponsors, Chairman, Chief Executive, Managing Director, elected Directors, by whatever name called, and guarantors of the company or body corporate or any one exercising direction or control of the affairs of such company or a body corporate; and in the case of any firm, partnership or sole proprietorship, the partners, proprietor or any person having any interest in the said firm, partnership or proprietorship concern or direction or control thereof.

The above definition of 'person' as revised by way of amendments, extends the scope of "corruption and corrupt practices" to corporate frauds and misappropriations. Accordingly, for corporate frauds and misappropriations, a special prosecution under the Ordinance of 1999 is attracted before the Accountability Courts, established pursuant to the Ordinance

---

8 Source: www.nab.gov.pk/Downloads/nao.asp#Corruption_12, accessed 19 November 2008.

EXHIBIT 7 (CONTINUED)

CASES IN CORPORATE GOVERNANCE 29

of 1999. Upon successful prosecution for the offense of corruption and corrupt practices, the delinquent corporate management may face rigorous imprisonment which may extend to fourteen years in addition to the payment of a fine and the confiscation of the property misappropriated or obtained through corruption and corrupt practices. The Ordinance of 1999 expressly provides that the imposition of fine as a punishment 'shall in no case be less than the gain derived by the accused ... by the commission of the offence.' The Ordinance of 1999 is the first-ever legislation in Pakistan that has treated a holder of a public office at par with the corporate management for the purposes of prosecution under the Ordinance of 1999. However, the Supreme Court of Pakistan has already considered an office of the public company to be a public office and, therefore, entertained constitutional petitions for the issuance of the writ of *quo-warranto*.[9]

Accordingly, the above jurisprudential expansion needs to be carefully reviewed keeping in view all the repercussions for the growing capital market in Pakistan.

---

9   In the United States today, quo warranto usually arises in a civil case as a plaintiff's claim (and thus a 'cause of action' instead of a writ) that some governmental or corporate official was not validly elected to that office or is wrongfully exercising powers beyond (or ultra vires) those authorized by statute or by the corporation's charter. In some jurisdictions which have enacted judicial review statutes, such as Queensland, the prerogative writ of quo warranto has been abolished.

1.2 CALLMATE TELIPS (B): ORIX INVESTMENT BANK PAKISTAN LIMITED—CALLMATE RISK UNCOVERED

CASE HIGHLIGHTS AND KEY POINTS

This case has been developed from information available in the public domain, mainly in the annual reports, and deals with the contrast between the code of corporate governance as stated by the company Orix Investment Bank Pakistan Limited (OIBPL) and the actual behaviour of company management when faced with difficult situations. The case follows the bank's performance over a number of years and focuses the analyst's attention to the astonishing fact that one single deal almost caused the bank to close. This is a follow up case to *Callmate Telips (A)—Choice of Accounting Policy*. The analyst while going through this case can examine the following:

1. The turmoil in 2008 in the world financial markets had one factor in common: there was a crisis of governance in corporations across the world. The OIBPL, being an investment bank, was closely related to the functioning of the Pakistan stock market being member of the Karachi Stock Exchange (KSE). The case shows that the bank's risk management function was so weak that as a result of one equity deal going bad, the OIBPL would have had to merge or go under, had it not been bailed out by the parent company in Japan.

2. An obligation of integrity, degree of professionalism, and transparency by the directors is required by all the stakeholders. While we cannot say that the directors were guilty of any crime, the circumstantial evidence in the case leads one to conjecture that by deciding to delay the provisioning of the huge write off related to the Callmate Telips Telecom Limited (CTTL) investment, they did not act professionally. This is confirmed by the fact that at the same time the papers were abuzz with news that the CTTL directors had been convicted in a criminal lawsuit. Another point is that how could the directors allow the deal to be done with CTTL, given all that was known about its fracas with its auditors and the regulator SECP (see *Callmate Telips (A) Choice of accounting policy*).

3. The Basel 2 framework (case EXHIBIT 1) for bank risk management clearly lays the responsibility on the Board to have managed the risks of the dealings with CTTL.

4. The audit committee is a key forum that should protect the company by ensuring checks on the acts of the board of directors through a regular feedback on decisions taken. In OIBPL the audit committee constituted half of the board of directors and there had been no change for many years in the members of this committee. Even after the bank undergoing a near financial disaster the directors remained the same. It is difficult for a director to be taking management decisions as well as auditing them critically!

5. The accounting policies adopted must follow generally accepted accounting practices, one of which is 'conservatism'. The provision of Rs. 426 million related to the CTTL diminution in value should have been made in the first quarter of 2008, if not earlier, instead of waiting until the end of 2008 when the external auditors would audit the financial statements. This raises the issue of the transparency of the board decisions.

6. The work of the auditors in issuing their verdict on compliance with the Code of Corporate Governance can also be reviewed. They did not mention in their 2007 report that the directors of CTTL were in court and this would have an impact on the CTTL share price and hence, it could have a significant impact on OIBPL profits. If they had examined the worst case scenario, that OIBPL would have to take up all the CTTL shares whose price was much below the acquisition cost and they would not have issued an unqualified report.

7. The regulator of investment banks and of the KSE was the Securities and Exchange Commission of Pakistan (SECP) while the State Bank of Pakistan regulated the commercial banks. The use of a type of financing for short selling called 'badla' and the fact that OIBPL was an active player in this highly speculative process, which though not illegal bordered on the unethical, should have been replaced with a documented and less risky arrangement by the two regulators as had been agreed in 2004. The Securities Commission in India had changed over from the 'badla' to a better financing mechanism in 1981.

POTENTIAL USES OF THE CASE

1. This case can be used in an MBA or a Senior Executive program to highlight the various pressures that make it difficult for the management to follow a framework of Corporate Governance. The case narrates albeit subtly how information was withheld from the stakeholders, ostensibly the only consideration being that the share price would tumble. Despite their reluctance the directors had to take the decision to write off a huge investment and as such there was no merit in delaying it.

2. It can also be used in a class on Business Ethics.

    2.1 The board of directors had let through their controls a transaction with a rogue company CTTL which was very circumlocutory in their wording on the huge loss, which they did not include in the half yearly performance report of 2008. It is almost certain that they knew that the directors of the company CTTL, whose shares the bank was holding, had been found guilty in a criminal case.

Management has to be judicious in disclosing information, but in OIBPL there was a huge loss that was delayed from being reported under the guise that efforts were being made to resolve the problem. It must have been known to the board of OIBPL that in November 2007 the verdict of the case against CTTL directors was clear: that directors were guilty of manipulating the share price. It was inconceivable for OIBPL to hope that CTTL shares would be of interest to anyone.

The two sets of investigations into the stock market crash had clearly implicated OIBPL as not acting in a professional manner and, in fact, were helping in the manipulation of CTTL share price by providing funding to investors that included members of the company board.

The core issue is how should the code of corporate governance (COCG), which is now required to be stated by all listed companies in their annual reports by the KSE regulations, be applied in actual day to day management. The case has the COCG whose clauses can be discussed vís-a-vís the management actions and the following aspects need consideration:

1. What is the responsibility of the company management to the community at large? This would decide whether the information is relayed in a shareholders meeting or via the press;

2. Balance between disclosing the facts as they occur and not releasing sensitive information that would have an adverse impact or to disclose limited amount.

3. Is it possible for the auditors to be able to give a separate opinion on the COCG? There are established auditing standards that govern an audit report but what criteria can the financial auditor use to pass judgment on the governance of a company?

The case clearly states that the deficit in the value of the CTTL shares was in excess of Rs. half a billion but was not passed through the income statement for the first half of 2008. The facts were that the arrangements for placements of CTTL shares were insecure (possibly done as private deals) so that OIBPL virtually ended up owning the shares of approximately Rs. 650 million (USD 1 = Rs. 65 in first half of 2008).

It is clear that the organizational structure of the risk assessment division of the bank was insufficient as it allowed a single exposure in an investment to be so large as to jeopardize the existence of the bank. The directors can be held to be at fault to have allowed this weakness in risk evaluation of the deal with CTTL. The charts show that CTTL share price over the three years was going in a downward direction. Earlier in 2006 it had been extremely volatile and trading was suspended (see case Callmate Telips Telecom Limited: Choice of Accounting Policy) especially when the news of insider trading surfaced. If the directors were unaware of what their staff was doing, that would be negligence and grounds for removal from the board. Ironically, no director was changed by the board as it carried out changes.

ASSIGNMENT QUESTIONS

1. What were the reasons that the directors refrained from making the Rs. half a billion provision for the diminution in value of CTTL shares in the 2008 half yearly report on OIBPL, and were they correct in their point of view?

2. Explain the purpose of the statement of the Code of Corporate Governance (COCG) in the Annual Report.

3. Evaluate the auditor's opinion on the COCG and state what do you understand by it? Are the auditors competent to give an opinion on the COCG in the case of OIBPL?

4. Why did OIBPL sign such a large agreement of Rs. 750 million with CTTL and what were the risks?

5. No board member was changed even though the bank was brought to its knees. Do you agree with this decision? Include in your answer what steps you would have taken?

CASE TEXT: CALLMATE TELIPS (B): ORIX INVESTMENT BANK PAKISTAN LIMITED—CALLMATE RISK UNCOVERED[1]

In October 2008, a financial analyst who was an investor on the Karachi Stock Exchange (KSE) was engrossed in reading the 30 June 2008 annual report of Orix Investment Bank Pakistan Limited (OIBPL). Parts of it appeared to be an Aesop's fable about the fundamental lapse in management control that almost led OIBPL into insolvency. Of particular interest was the statement relating to Special Business under S160 (1) (b) of the Companies Ordinance, 1984. This said that the financial performance of the bank had suffered in the last two years due to the share trading transaction of Callmate Telips Telecom Limited (CTTL). As a consequence, the net equity of the company as at 30 June 2008, stood at Rs. 419 million, which was less than the Rs. 500 million required by the new Non Bank Financial Companies rules. This shortfall was mainly due to the provisioning against CTTL shares of Rs. 639 million. A further injection of equity was required, failing which the bank would continue to be in breach of the minimum equity requirement.

The analyst recalled that at the end of 2004 the stock prices in the KSE had crashed across the board. The key KSE-100 Index then increased by 65 per cent, from 6,218 on 31 December 2004, to 10,303 on 15 March 2005. Subsequently, two sets of investigations had been done by the government and one of these stated that Orix Investment Bank Pakistan Ltd was among the brokers who accounted for approximately 50 per cent of the total value of Badla purchases occurring between 3 January 2005 and 15 March 2005. In October 2006, CTTL had given a mandate to OIBPL as its financial advisor to arrange 'Badla' financing for transactions valuing Rs. 750 million of Callmate shares. According to the mandate, OIBPL would advise and assist CTTL in the designing, structuring, and undertaking of book-building exercises and placement of a large block of common equity shares for Callmate accumulating to Rs. 750 million. The OIBIL would also act as the placement agent and book-building agent for the entire Badla financing on behalf of CTTL and diversify the distribution of offerings that included the retail and institutional investors base. As OIBPL was the financial advisor of CTTL, if appropriate and if so required it would also undertake designing, distributing and structuring a Badla[2] financing for CTTL. CTTL had paid 1.5 per cent of Rs. 750 million as the advisory fee to the financial advisor.

---

1   This case has been written on the basis of published sources only. Consequently, the interpretation and perspectives presented in this case are not necessarily those of Orix Investment Bank Pakistan Limited or any of its employees.

2   'Badla' is essentially a facility for financing share purchases extended by brokerages and banks which allows buyers to obtain

It now appeared that the CTTL transaction had gone sour and the bank had somehow ended up with almost all the Callmate shares whose price on 30 June 2008, had fallen to Rs. 1.4. This was a disaster compared to the earlier price height of Rs. 109 that the share had touched. The analyst wanted to know how OIBPL, an investment bank with international shareholders and with a stated code of governance, had dealt with the highly risky Badla financing and how it could make a decision that almost lead it to bankruptcy. He was concerned about the quality of information provided to stakeholders and the period during which there had been no change in members of the board of directors, and decided to investigate this major but disastrous investment by OIBPL.

BACKGROUND

ORIX Investment Bank Pakistan Limited (OIBPL) was a joint venture sponsored by ORIX Corporation, Japan. Other major shareholders (see Exhibit 1) were:

1. ORIX Leasing Pakistan Limited

2. International Finance Corporation

3. Asian Finance & Investment Corporation

4. Saudi Pak Industrial & Agricultural Investment Company (Private) Limited

5. Pak Kuwait Investment Company (Private) Limited

---

highly leveraged positions in the market. A brokerage client can delay the payment for purchases indefinitely by paying Badla overnight finance rates via an overnight sale and buy-back mechanism. The extent of leverage through such non-bank financing for Badla is not transparent and underlying security transactions are typically speculative. A feature of this short-term finance provision is that a large proportion of funding comes from insurance and mutual funds. This accentuates the risk for both investors and users of Badla finance. In addition, Badla also creates scope for market manipulation and increases systemic risk.

Example—Investor: Badla investor wishes to lend money to BUY overnight shares at a price that should give a return about four to five per cent above short-term rates. At the same time as the BUY, they execute a next day SELL contract for the same parcel.

Example—Speculator: Market holder cannot fund a shareholding so they overnight SELL to a Badla investor at a cost of carry four to five per cent above short-term rates. At the same time, they execute a next day BUY contract for the same parcel of shares.

OIBPL was initially incorporated as a Public Limited Company under the name of ORIX Investment Finance Company Pakistan Limited in July 1995 and was listed in the Karachi and Lahore Stock Exchanges. The bank claimed to only work with high net-worth individuals, entrepreneurs, rapidly growing companies, multinationals, financial institutions, public sector corporations and government agencies. Its areas of service and operations initially were:

- Corporate finance

- Credit and marketing

- Money market and equity brokerage services

- Treasury operations

The equity division of OIBPL started its operation in 2004. The division was created to respond to the expected rise in interest rates and hence narrowing of margins in lending activities. Thus, there was a need to diversify and benefit from other emerging opportunities in the capital market of Pakistan. The equity division became a major contributor to the bank's profitability and in a short period evolved into a leading brokerage house providing a spectrum of services to numerous institutions and high net-worth individuals. The division staff felt that it was spearheading the bank's effort to support and develop Pakistan's capital market. The division had been innovative and besides providing equity sales and research, it had provided Badla fund placement and hedging solutions to the clients. The division also pursued arbitrage opportunities and intended to serve all premier financial institutions such as DFIs, mutual funds, banks, and NBFIs for their capital market needs. It was supported by the research department and a professional team of four equity dealers backed by a strong back office settlement team. The equity brokerage department provided the following services:

1. Cross exchange trading

2. Arbitrage transactions

3. Securities lending/borrowing

4. Private asset management advisory services

5. Non-discretionary accounts trading for individuals

6. Margin trading

7. Placement of block sales for corporate and high net-worth clients

8. Futures trading

9. Underwriting

OIBPL OPERATIONS IN RECENT YEARS

The bank had acquired an equity brokers' license on the Karachi Stock Exchange (Guarantee) Limited through competitive bidding, as the management expected this new investment to reap good profits in a booming market. In 2004, the long-term prospects of the bank had improved further with the commencement of equity brokerage operations, which were in full swing. This division was contributing towards the non-fund as well as the fund-based activities with growing potential. The increase in administrative and operating expenses was almost entirely due to the expenses directly related to the equity brokerage division which had started contributing to the profitability of the bank. Based on the results for the year ended 30 June 2004, Pakistan Credit Rating Agency (PACRA) had maintained the company's long-term and short-term entity ratings at 'A' (Single A) and 'A1' (A One), respectively.

During 2005, the bank achieved a nine per cent increase in its net profit. It now had diverse sources of revenue from all segments of the capital market. Despite stiff competition from commercial banks, OIBPL succeeded in expanding both its fund-based and advisory businesses. The addition of equity brokerage to its services was also bearing fruit. The pre-tax profit of the bank increased to Rs. 177 million from the previous year's Rs. 163 million (see Exhibit 2) and the after tax profit to Rs. 166 million from Rs. 116 million. The gross revenues from loans and investments had increased from Rs. 273 million to Rs. 350 million. The borrowing costs went up from Rs. 98 million to Rs. 163 million as a sequel to an increase in investments and also because of rising interest rates. The biggest increase, however, was in the non-fund based fee income going from Rs. 54 million to Rs. 127 million. The administrative expenses increased to Rs. 108 million from Rs. 62 million in the previous year as the costs included the first full year's cost.

REGULATORY CHANGES

The factors being faced by investment banks were: (i) consistency of government policies; (ii) elimination of the irritant relating to renewal of license on a yearly basis; (iii) resolution of issues arising out of the accounting policies for new investment banking products; (iv) enforcement of quality governance at the stock exchanges; (v) an early resolution of the long outstanding issue of rate of taxation; and (vi) the imperative of a 'level playing field' and the uniform 'application of specialized regulation.'

The OIBPL board of directors had remained unchanged for the last six years and the audit committee, which consisted of three board directors, also remained unchanged in the same period. It appeared that the concept espoused by ORIX Corporation Japan (see Exhibit 1) was not implemented by OIBPL. The bank management considered brokerage to be the most important activity for the functioning of the capital markets and a legitimate business activity for investment banks the world over. Hence there was a rising trend of investment banks taking up brokerage activities and even a number of conventional brokerage houses had voluntarily embraced a corporate structure. This was a healthy trend, as these institutions were properly rated, regulated, documented, and had high levels of compliance with regulatory and corporate governance standards. OIBPL had detailed in the annual report its code of corporate governance (see Exhibit 3) and it appeared different from the Orix Corporation Japan corporate governance concepts. However, the auditor's report on the compliance with the code gave OIBPL a clean report (see Exhibit 4). The style of the report followed that of the report on the financial statements but it did not make it clear what work had been done to prepare the report.

KSE Market Crash

In March 2005, the Karachi Stock Exchange witnessed an unusual increase in the index such that within a span of three months the share index had risen by 65 per cent. As per the agreement in 2004 between the SECP (Securities and Exchange Commission of Pakistan) and the KSE management, Badla, also known as Carry Over Transaction (COT), was planned to have been phased out. The phasing out of Badla would have led to the replacement of the traditional scheme with a margin financing scheme through banks and financial institutions. However, the big brokerage houses, which were also financers of the Badla system, created a panic-like situation by suddenly stopping Badla financing before the system was fully phased out. Prior to the crisis, the market was artificially increased to very high levels. The key KSE-100 Index increased by 65 per cent, from 6,218 on 31 December 2004 to 10,303 on 15 March 2005. This market surge created a frenzied panic in the market. However, the sudden stoppage of Badla finances hit small investors hard, especially those who had bought large quantities of shares anticipating the appreciation of share values against Badla financing. They could not get the financing to settle their holdings and thus incurred huge losses.

After the crash, the State Bank of Pakistan (SBP) in its 2006 annual review of the performance of financial markets had suggested to policy makers that Badla financing in share markets be completely 'removed with better risk management tools'. It further said, 'Few (stock) brokers can still maneuver the market.' The central bank which regulated the commercial banks, but not investment banks said the March 2005 crisis hinted towards market manipulation. Though the number of investors had grown tremendously over the years, few big brokers could still manoeuvre the market. The SBP said another factor instilling instability in equity markets was the presence of Badla or COT financing which, it said 'supports speculative activities without proper exposure.'

The amount of losses of investors was estimated to be in the billions of rupees and the government was under a lot of public pressure to launch an inquiry to determine if the market had been manipulated, as was the belief of many stakeholders. The SECP, being the primary regulator of the stock market, undertook two sets of inquiries whose results are summarized below.

FIRST INVESTIGATION—THE TASK FORCE REPORT

In its June 2005 (the *Task Force Report*) report, Justice (Retd.) Saleem Akhtar's task force had concluded that the rise and fall of the stock market in March 2005 was at least partly attributable to a number of manipulative activities, schemes, and market abuses involving unnamed brokers.

The alleged scheme's key components were:

1. First, certain brokers had conspired to use manipulative trading practices to drive scrip prices up. They created artificial euphoria and overly optimistic sentiments through wash trades[3] and misleading statements, which had attracted additional investors into the market and had driven scrip prices even higher.

2. These brokers had liberally supplied a large volume of Badla for the heightened demand in trading, which further escalated prices and also permitted smaller investors to take on highly leveraged positions. They later systematically restricted Badla availability, sending share-hungry, weak investors to the futures counter.

3. As scrip prices rose, the brokers locked in those (inflated) prices by selling heavily in the March futures contracts and further complicated the scenario by selling shares they did not actually own, fully intending to defer the acquisition of those shares to a later date to benefit from anticipated price declines.

4. At a later stage, these same brokers then adversely influenced the market's liquidity through additional Badla restrictions, which had the effect of stalling the market, and this sent scrip prices downward. Brokers then purchased the requisite shares in the Ready Market, at highly discounted prices, to satisfy delivery of setoff shares in settlement of their March futures sales contracts and made hefty profits in the process.

5. Finally, in order to prevent massive defaults by buyers stuck with open futures contracts, these same brokers persuaded regulators to create special trading periods and to extend the normal settlement period by three days to allow the brokers to provide additional Badla funding to futures contract holders.

---

3   A wash trade is a buy-and-sell transaction between colluding persons that simply increases the volumes of shares traded whereas in fact no arms-length deal took place.

The task force acknowledged that the enormity of the task of analysing the various factors associated with the market's fall in March 2005 necessitated a much longer and more thorough investigation. Its effort was complicated, both by the massive volume of data that had to be examined, and by the inherent limitations of that data.

Accordingly, the task force called on the SECP to conduct a follow-on forensic investigation of the most material alleged abuses.

SECOND INVESTIGATION—DILIGENCE REPORT

This investigation was conducted by a firm from the United States known as Diligence, which was asked to look into the events of March 2005 at the KSE and submitted its report on 21 November 2006.

Its forensic report pointed out a violation of the rules under Clause 3(b) of the *Regulations Governing Futures Contracts* and Section 17(a) of the *Securities and Exchange Ordinance*. This clause prohibited a broker from having a net sale position in future contracts of particular scrip in excess of Rs. 50 million without providing evidence that he or she held the shares sold above the threshold.

The U.S. company's forensic report had also agreed to the role of Badla in the market crash and the possible wrongdoing of 13 brokers. Justice (Retd.) Saleem Akhtar's task force report had pointed fingers at 11 brokers. According to the forensic report, trading data analysis had revealed that most of the brokers trading on the KSE participated in the Badla market. However, daily new Badla transactions on the KSE were heavily concentrated with relatively few brokers. Of the 138 brokers participating in the Badla market on behalf of lenders, six brokers accounted for approximately 50 per cent of the total value of Badla purchases occurring between 3 January 2005 and 15 March 2005. In order of descending new Badla values, the five brokers were: Aqeel Karim Dhedhi Securities (Pvt.) Ltd, Arif Habib Securities Limited, Atlas Capital Markets (Pvt.) Limited, KASB Securities Limited, and Orix Investment Bank Pakistan Ltd. The three brokers Akberally Cassim & Sons., Aqeel Karim Dhedhi Securities and Arif Habib Securities together represented close to 30 per cent of the total new Badla lending market during that period.

The Diligence report disputed many findings of the task force report regarding the role of the major brokerage houses and their Badla financing in the crash. The forensic report stated: 'We do not find sufficient evidence to support the paramount scheme of manipulation in the manner put forth by the task force for the period in question. Nor do we find sufficient evidence to support the alleged scheme's primary element (withdrawal of Badla), that was ostensibly responsible for the fall of market prices. We find no patterns of activity or credible evidence to support a theory that, during March 2005, certain influential brokers systematically and manipulatively inflated and then deflated market prices, reaping substantial profits in the process.'

Investigation of Callmate Share Dealings

In 2006, an investigation by the SECP into trades of CTTL shares, specifically during the period between 31 December 2005 and 30 June 2006, produced surprising findings as to the nature and extent of the company directors' manipulation of the share price for their gain. The SECP was alerted when it saw the pattern of repeated lower and upper locks during trading. Consequent to the unusual trading behavior in the shares of Callmate Telips Telecom Company Ltd. (CTTL), the Securities & Exchange Commission of Pakistan (the Commission) initiated an investigation into the matter.

From an analysis of the trading data (reviewed at a broker level as well as the client level) using the Universal Identification Number database, it appeared that a group of persons (the Group) acting in concert and including key officials of CTTL as well as members of the Ansari family (members of the CTTL board), were involved in insider trading and price manipulation of CTTL shares.

On one hand, the price of scrip was escalated by buying large quantities of scrip on upticks, whereas on the other hand an artificial turnover was generated by buying and selling CTTL shares within the Group. The price of the scrip was manipulated by placing abnormal bids (upper locks) and offers (lower locks) during pre-open sessions. Shares were bought from various brokerage houses and financing was obtained through the COT market. By generating artificial turnover as well as manipulating prices upward and downward, profits were generated which were then used to acquire fresh CTTL shares. Furthermore, COT was rolled over on a daily basis and paper profits extracted at the expense of the COT market.

As a result of these prohibited activities, by 8 December 2006, the Group had acquired 80.95 per cent of the share capital of CTTL.

Some brokerage houses especially Orix Investment Bank, First National Equities Ltd., First Pakistan Securities Limited, and Al-Hoqani Securities, had also played an active role in the affair. They had been found to have assisted the Group to actively manipulate the market. These houses, despite having knowledge that major shareholders and insiders of the company were involved in the trading of CTTL shares, acted on their behalf and assisted them in the following acts:

- Engaging in a series of transactions that were reported on a public display facility to give the impression of activity or price movement in the security;

- Transactions in which there was no change in beneficial ownership of the security; i.e. *wash sales*;

- Transactions where both buy and sell orders were entered at the same time, with the same price and quantity by different but colluding parties;

- Increasing the bid for a security to increase its price; i.e buying on uptick, thus manipulating the price;

- Buying at increasingly higher prices, and then selling in the market (often to retail customers) at the higher prices (*pumping and dumping*);

- Assisting in avoiding disclosure requirements under Sec. 4 of the *Listed Companies (Substantial Acquisitions of voting shares and takeovers) Ord, 2002* by splitting the purchase of one member of the Group into a purchase by two members of the Group;

- Arranging financing for the Group for acquiring a large number of the company's shares.

The share price movements of CTTL for the three years from 2006 to 2008 are shown in Exhibit 5.

During 2006, the bank achieved a substantial 22 per cent increase in its net profit. It now had diverse sources of revenue from all segments of the capital market. The equity brokerage services generated Rs. 178 million in revenue, up from Rs. 127 million the previous year. The pre-tax profit of the bank increased to Rs. 216 million from the previous year's Rs. 177 million. The borrowing costs went up from Rs. 163 million to Rs. 304 million as a sequel to an increase in investments and also because of rising interest rates. The administrative expenses increased to Rs. 141 million from Rs. 108 million in the previous year, as the cost was accounted for by the equity brokerage business.

EQUITY DIVISION SUFFERS A MAJOR SETBACK

The financial year 2007 proved to be a difficult year for OIBPL as the bank's operations suffered a major setback stemming from a shares financing transaction. The transaction, mainly originated with the brokerage division, related to certain clients and linked to a single scrip: Callmate Telips Telecommunication Limited (CTTL). The bank had to pay off the respective liabilities and these shares were eventually transferred to OIBL's proprietary investment portfolio. While the management failed to reach a settlement with respective clients, the value of these shares deteriorated significantly compared to their cost of acquisition, resulting in a substantial loss for the bank. The share prices at the end of each quarter of financial year 2007 were:

Quarter 1 30 Sept. 2006	Half Year 30 Dec. 2006	Quarter 3 30 March 2007	Year End 30 June 2007
Rs. 46.40 per share	Trading Suspended	Rs. 44.15 per share	Rs. 49.50 per share

The reasons for suspension of the share trading in CTTL shares (refer to *Callmate Telips (A)—Choice of Accounting Policy* do not seem to have affected the bank management. However the transaction relating to CTTL shares was so large that it affected other areas of operations adversely, as reflected by subdued performance of the bank across various segments, especially brokerage and other fee-based services. Consequently, income from non-fund based operations—historically the major contributor towards the bottom line— declined substantially (around 34 per cent) during the year; it fell to Rs. 119 million from Rs. 178 million in 2006. However, the management expressed its resolve to continue to pursue the said receivables and had not forfeited its claim over the amounts owed.

The balance written off was Rs. 255 million, which represented the difference between the total receivable amount and the market value of the ordinary shares on the date of transfer to the proprietary investment account of the company. Other customers on the same trades owed Rs. 135 million, but that was not covered by provision as it was considered good debt.

During the year the bank's equity was seriously eroded due to accumulated losses and its capital adequacy ratios were also not as was required by the SECP. The board of directors recognized the situation and conducted a right issue of 200 per cent, which generated Rs. 726 million as capital to mitigate the financial losses and enhance the equity base of the bank. Although the increase in capital enhanced the risk absorption capacity of the bank, the ensuing loss in the investment portfolio further eroded it, necessitating the need for another round of capitalization. The overall financial portfolio of the bank also reduced slightly. OIBPL continued with its money and capital market financing operations but there was a significantly higher finance cost, as the bank had to revert to short-term borrowings to finance its operations—including financing for transacted shares—and this led to reduced interest revenue.

The chairman in his report said: 'The system of internal controls is sound in design and has been effectively implemented and monitored with the exception of the matters referred in note 32 to the financial statements of the current year.' The note 32 mentioned in summarized manner that certain customers had defaulted from taking up the CTTL shares which they had contracted to buy and hence a receivable of Rs. 255 million had to be written off, as OIBPL was obliged to pay off the borrowing with which the Badla transactions had been financed. In addition to the monetary losses, OIBL's reputation was also damaged by the transaction. The management revamped its organizational structure and most of the top management team excluding any director, was replaced, though it found it difficult to fulfill all its HR requirements. The OIBPL annual report stated that OIBPL had also reviewed its risk management systems and control mechanism at various organizational levels. It appears that the transactions had most probably not been done through the KSE but instead were deals made unofficially. This would mean that there was some level of collusion between senior officers of OIBPL and Callmate directors.

OIBPL investment in CTTL shares was in serious jeopardy, as in April 2007 SECP completed the investigation of the share dealings of CTTL and lodged a case in court against the management of CTTL. On 11 November 2007, the court ordered the issuance of bailable warrants against the directors of Callmate Telips Telecom Limited (CTTL) for indulging in wash trades, circular trades, insider trading and other manipulative practices in CTTL shares.

As reported by the *Business Recorder*, in his order issued by Third Additional Session Judge Karachi South, Sultan Muhammad Awan ruled that the accused persons created the false and misleading appearance of active trading in CTTL shares with a view to raising the price of CTTL shares for inducing purchase by the public at large and also sold CTTL shares to make unlawful gains.

In addition, the press reported that the order said, 'The accused persons used price sensitive insider information to indulge in trading in CTTL shares. Prima facie offence under section 15-A and Section 17 punishable under section 15B (4) and Section 24 read with 25 is made out against the accused persons.' While adjourning the proceedings to 24 November, the court went on to say: 'Register the complaint, issue bailable warrants against each of the accused persons in the sum of Rs. 100,000 with one surety and PR bond in the like amount each in terms of section 265-C *Criminal Penal Code*. The complainant shall supply a complete set of the complaints to the accused persons in court.'

The court order said that the complaint and the SECP report (*Investigation Report: Callmate Telips Telecommunication Co. Ltd, For the Period 7 November 2006 to 8 December 2006*) had discovered an unusual trading pattern in the trading of CTTL shares. 'It is also mentioned in paragraph 14 of the complaint that the changed trading pattern was ascertained by comparing the average daily turnover of CTTL shares during the subject period which increased to 4,680,000 shares against the average daily turnover of 1,713,367 shares during the preceding 12 months period,' the court order said, and added that the SECP as per the law held an inquiry into the affairs and dealings in CTTL shares on the Karachi Stock Exchange.

Some brokerage firms, especially Orix Investment Bank, First National Equities Ltd, First Pakistan Securities Limited, and Al-Hoqani Securities, had also played an active role in this affair. They had been found to be assisting the Group in actively manipulating the market. These firms, despite having knowledge that major shareholders and insiders of the company were involved in trading of CTTL shares, acted on their behalf and assisted them in engaging in a series of transactions that were reported on a public display facility to give the impression of activity or price movement in the security:

1. Transactions in which there was no change in beneficial ownership of the security; i.e., wash sales—transactions where both buy and sell orders were entered at the same time, with the same price and quantity by different but colluding parties;

2. Increasing the bid for a security to increase its price; i.e., buying on uptick, thus manipulating the price; buying at increasingly higher prices, and then selling in the market (often to retail customers) at the higher prices (pumping and dumping).

These firms had also assisted in avoiding disclosure requirements under Sec. 4 of the *Listed Companies (Substantial Acquisitions of voting shares and take-overs) Ord, 2002* by splitting a purchase of one member of the Group into a purchase by two members of the Group; and arranging financing for the Group for further acquisition of the company's shares.

According to the inquiry team, these brokerage firms were also found violating various rules and regulations namely *Brokers and Agents Registration Rules, 2001*; *KATS Regulations, General Rules & Regulations*; etc. Likewise, Orix Investment Bank Pakistan Limited (OIBPL) at one instance, when buying for its client Asim Fayyaz Qureshi, exceeded the threshold of 10 per cent of outstanding capital of CTTL and divided the buying of 5,844,500 shares between two of its clients, Ajmal Ansari, CEO of CTTL, and Asim Fayyaz Qureshi, to avoid disclosure under *Listed Companies (Substantial Acquisitions of voting shares and take-overs) Ord, 2002* and the *Companies Ordinance 1984*. Based on the SECP inquiry team's review of the data and records, there existed prima facie evidence that potential violation of various laws, rules, regulations, and guidelines was committed by the accused persons.

In the first half of the year 2008, the bank posted positive earnings as the management did not recognize the further deficit in the value of CTTL shares (Rs. 465 million) as a provision, as this would have reported a loss for the period. Instead it chose to show the loss as a contra against equity under the heading: 'Deficit on revaluation of securities amounting to Rs. 501 million' (see Exhibit 4).

On this accounting method, the auditors review simply stated, 'The investments in shares of Callmate Telips Telecommunication Company Limited (CTTL) have been classified as

"Available for sale" with deficit in mark to market amounting to Rs. 456.922 million was not considered as impairment and was taken to "Deficit on revaluation of securities" in Balance Sheet. The management considers that the decline in market value is temporary. We understand that the investees' operations have significantly curtailed and the latest audited financial statements for the year ended 30 June 2007 show poor operating performance and unsatisfactory financial position. Accordingly, we consider that a valuation and full due diligence exercise should be carried out to determine the extent of impairment. In the absence of such an exercise we are unable to determine the extent of impairment and its effect on profit and loss account.'[4]

OIBL's management explored options to dispose of its stake in CTTL, but under the circumstances where the directors of CTTL had been issued warrants for arrest on charge of fraudulent dealing in CTTL shares, there would be no buyers and losses from these shares would materialize. The share price of Callmate Telips Telecom Limited (CTTL) had been constantly on the decline. As a consequence, the deficit on the revaluation of securities on account of its shares had increased to Rs. 456.9 million. As highlighted by the auditors in their review (item 1.2) and further explained in notes to the accounts, efforts were underway to restart CTTL's suspended operations. If these efforts had succeeded then some of the lost value may have been recovered. The management thus had no option but to fully provide for the impairment in the current financial year. Initially, the decline in the value of this investment was being reported as a deficit on the revaluation of securities. If the deficit had been written off or provided for, the bank's loss for the 2008 half-year would have been Rs. 424.4 million.

The directors of OIBPL did not mention the court case against the majority of the board of directors of CTTL in the 2007 or 2008 annual reports. In the 2007 report, they wrote that they felt sorry to inform the shareholders of grievous setback to the working of their bank in the fiscal year ended 30 June 2007. It was caused in transacting share business with some clients representing a single party. The huge and adverse impact of the transaction on the income of the bank, the actions taken to minimize it, and the measures in hand to restore the prestige and profit of the bank were never explained.

During 2008, the bank all along had to contend with the serious setback it suffered in the

---

4   Source: Company half-yearly report (Unaudited), *Business Recorder*, 31 December 2007.

previous year's trading transaction in the shares of CTTL. In February 2008, CTTL had announced its delayed accounts for the financial year 2007. The company posted a net loss of Rs. 359 million (loss per share Rs. 5.50) compared with a profit of Rs. 603 million (earning per share Rs. 9.23) in the year preceding. The CTTL share price had fallen drastically:

Quarter 1 30 Sept 2007	Half Year 30 Dec 2007	Quarter 3 30 March 2008	Year End 30 June 2008
Rs. 42.97 per share	Rs. 14.85 per share	Rs. 6.59 per share	Rs. 2.00 per share

As the market value deteriorated and no buyer of the Callmate shares could be found, the stuck-up shares had to be included as OIBPL's proprietary investment. The management's efforts to recoup the losses suffered due to this transaction could not succeed; it was then decided to provide for the total cost and unrealized loss of CTTL shares amounting to Rs. 625.971 million. As a consequence the net equity of the bank as at 30 June 2008 stood reduced to Rs. 419.889 million.

To add to the bank's woes, even the normal business of the bank was affected due to the depression both in the investment activities and in the stock market. The increase in the discount rate by the State Bank to contain inflation led to higher interest rates which increased the cost of borrowings. Political uncertainty and economic slump had combined to dampen investments in capital markets. Falling trading volumes in stocks had drastically reduced the revenue of the equity brokerage division.

RIGHTS ISSUE

During 2007, the bank issued 200 per cent right shares at par to bring the bank's paid-up capital to Rs. 1,089 million. The proceeds of the issue were realized in December 2007, but the enhanced capital had been eroded due to the provisioning of CTTL shares.

A further rights issue in the ratio of one share for every 1.452 shares held was planned. This rights issue, too, would be at par value, i.e., Rs. 10. This would bring in fresh capital of Rs. 750 million into the bank. ORIX Corporation, Japan, besides committing to take up its own share of entitlement, had agreed to underwrite the balance portion of the right shares.

The external auditors KPMG in their report on the 2008 financial statements referred to note 4 (see Exhibit 6) and said:

'Without qualifying our opinion, we draw attention to the following matters:

1. As mentioned in note 4.1 to the financial statements, the equity of the Company as at 30 June 2008 was less than minimum equity requirement of Rs. 500 million as specified in the Non-Banking Finance Companies and Notified Entities Regulations, 2007.

2. As mentioned in note 4.2 to the financial statements, the Company is not in compliance with regulation no. 28 of Non-Banking Finance Companies and Notified Entities Regulations, 2007 (NBFC).

The financial statements of the Company for the year ended 30 June 2007 were audited by another firm of Chartered Accountants who had modified their opinion with an emphasis of matter paragraph in their report dated 24 September 2007 in respect of Company's non-compliance with the Non-Banking Finance Companies (Establishment and Regulations) Rules, 2003 and Prudential Regulations for Non-Banking Finance Companies.'

It appeared that for 2008, the external auditors, KPMG, had relied upon the note 1.2 (see Exhibit 6) included in the annual report to issue an unqualified opinion on the financial statements. However, the various findings of the investigations and the court case convictions seemed to have been ignored, as the auditors had given an unqualified report on the bank's financials and compliance with the code of corporate governance (see Exhibit 7).

The analyst was surprised at how blatant and widespread the manipulation was of the share price of CTTL and that an organization such as OIBPL was involved in taking huge risks. He wondered if the only solution was for the regulator to prescribe in detailed governance parameters such as restricting the number of family members who could serve concurrently. He was considering writing a report which would try to clear the confusion that had engulfed investors since the small individual investors who had invested on the KSE did not understand the effect of Badla on the market.

EXHIBIT 1

CASES IN CORPORATE GOVERNANCE   53

ORIX JAPAN CORPORATE GOVERNANCE CONCEPTS

Since the June 1997 establishment of an Advisory Board, which included experienced and resourceful individuals from outside the Company, ORIX has strengthened its corporate governance framework with the aim of objectively determining whether its business activities are emphasizing the interests of its shareholders.

In June 1998, we introduced a Corporate Executive Officer system to help separate strategic decision-making functions from day-to-day administrative operations. In June 1999, ORIX reduced the number of members on its Board of Directors, arranged for three Advisory Board members to fill two positions as independent directors and one position as an advisor to the Board and phased out the Advisory Board. In addition, the Nominating Committee and the Compensation Committee were established to operate as support units for the Board of Directors.

To ensure the more effective separation and speedy execution of the decision-making and monitoring functions of the Board of Directors and the executive function of management, ORIX adopted a 'Company with Committees' board model in June 2003, following the April 2003 implementation of revisions to the Commercial Code of Japan that permit this model. In line with the new board model, nominating, audit, and compensation committees were set up. When the Company Law took effect on 1 May 2006, ORIX became a company with a revised 'Company with Committees' board model under that law.

There were five outside directors following the Annual General Meeting of Shareholders held on 24 June 2008, and all five seats on the nominating committee have been filled by outside directors since June 2007. As a result, all three committees-including the nominating, audit, and compensation committees are now comprised entirely of outside directors. ORIX believes that changing the membership composition in this manner will promote increased management transparency and objectivity.

EXHIBIT 1 (CONTINUED)

Orix Group Company's Shareholding

Direct holding of associated companies in the ordinary shares of Rs. 10/- each is as follows:

ORIX Corporation—Japan	32.51%
Leasing Pakistan Limited	15.00%
Asian Finance & Investment Corporation	7.50%
Pak Kuwait Investment Company (Private) Limited	4.98%
Saudi Pak Industrial & Agricultural Investment Company (Private) Limited	3.03%
Total	63.02%

Source: Company Annual Reports and ORIX, Japan website.

EXHIBIT 2

ORIX INVESTMENT BANK PAKISTAN LIMITED
FINANCIAL STATISTICS

PROFIT AND LOSS ACCOUNT		Half year of 2008				Rupees in millions	
FOR YEAR ENDED JUNE 30	2008		2007	2006	2005	2004	2003
INCOME							
Income from loans, term finances and credit facilities	262	209	401	323	148	110	194
Income from investments	151	117	151	208	202	162	185
Fee, commission and brokerage	58	21	119	178	127	54	36
Other income	12			0	0	1	2
	482	347	671	709	476	327	417
EXPENDITURE							
Return/mark-up on certificates of investment and borrowings	402	220	453	304	163	98	194
Receivables written off			255				
Diminution in investments	639						
Administrative and operating expenses	155	70	183	141	108	62	53
	1196	290	892	445	272	160	246
(Loss) Profit before provision and taxation	(714)	57	(221)	264	205	167	171
Provision for losses on term finances/credit facilities	59	(10)	(120)	48	28	3	26
(Loss) Profit before taxation	**(655)**	**47**	**(341)**	**216**	**177**	**163**	**145**
Provision for taxation—current	(10)	(14)	28	14	10	47	48
(Loss) Profit after taxation	(665)	33	(313)	202	167	116	97

BALANCE SHEETS		Half year of 2008			Rupees in millions		
FOR YEAR ENDED JUNE 30	2008		2007	2006	2005	2004	2003
ASSETS							
Non current assets							
Fixed assets	38	40	39	32	21	13	13
Stock exchange membership	81	81	81	74	42		
Long-term loans & term finances	389	426	431	386	432		336
Other assets	130	104	102	57	49	335	1
Sub-total	638	651	653	549	544	348	349
Current assets							
Short-term investments	1,301	1,610	1,598	1,120	1,086	1,536	1,696
Fund placements	314	1,607	1,845	1,947	25	160	753
Other assets	748	741	1,017	1,052	1,118	829	74
Cash and bank	267	282	238	395	543	91	91
Sub-total	2,629	4,240	4,698	4,514	2,772	2,616	2,615
	3,267	**4,891**	**5,351**	**5,062**	**3,316**	**2,964**	**2,964**
EQUITIES							
Share capital & reserves							
Paid in capital	1,089	1,089	363	363	330	300	300
Reserves	196	185	185				
Accumulated (losses) reserves	(865)	(168)	(201)	425	321	99	99
Net capital and reserves	420	1,106	347	788	651	399	399
Surplus (deficit) on revaluation	(95)	(501)**	(25)	(57)	-20	69	69
Net shareholder equity	325	605	322	731	631	468	468
Non current liabilities							
Long-term deposits and loans	717	770	926	323	642	235	235
Current liabilities							
Current maturity loans and short-term deposits	367	918	1,592	1,670	1,484	852	853
Short-term borrowings	1751	2,448	2,335	2,205	500	1,261	1,266
Other liabilities	107	150	176	134	60	148	142
Total current liabilities	2225	3,516	4,103	4,009	2,044	2,261	2,261
Total equities	**3,267**	**4,891**	**5,351**	**5,062**	**3,316**	**2,964**	**2,964**

** See Exhibit 4.

EXHIBIT 2 (CONTINUED)

CASES IN CORPORATE GOVERNANCE   57

The investment and reserves related to CTTL were shown as below:

Particulars of investment by segment					Rupees in millions	
	2008		2007		2006	
	Cost	Market	Cost	Market	Cost	Market
Government securities	692	557	363	300	377	307
Ordinary shares*	305	261	1,026	760	407	398
Term finance certificates	160	160	201	157	232	191
Open end mutual funds	.	210	125	169	120	130
Closed end mutual funds	128	108	136	127	57	50
	1,284	1,296	1,850	1,512	1,194	1,077
*Callmate ordinary shares	NIL	0	865	610	8	6
Unit share value		Rs. 2.00	Rs. 70.34	Rs. 49.50	Rs. 76.28	Rs. 55.50

CONTINGENCIES AND COMMITMENTS	2008	2008	2007	2006	2005	2004	Rupees in millions 2003
Contingencies		Half year					
Guarantees issued on behalf of customers	0	3	3	4	4	14	49
Letters of comfort on behalf of customers	35	110	110		100		
	35	113	113	4	104	14	49
Commitments							
Sale of equity securities under future contracts	105	127	88	93			
Purchase commitments under reverse repurchase agreements for shares	105	137	421	1,267	15		
Under reverse repurchase agreements of shares	77	1,259	1,211	1,272	305		
Capital expenditures			1	3	1		
	287	1,523	1,721	2,635	321	0	0

Source: Company Annual Reports.

STATEMENT OF COMPLIANCE WITH THE CODE OF CORPORATE GOVERNANCE FOR THE YEAR ENDED 30 JUNE 2008

Statement of Compliance

This statement of compliance is being presented to comply with the Code of Corporate Governance contained in listing regulations of Karachi and Lahore Stock Exchanges for the purpose of establishing a framework of good governance, whereby a listed company is managed in compliance with the best practices for the listed companies. The said Code has also been adopted by State Bank of Pakistan and stock exchanges. The Board of Directors of ORIX Investment Bank Pakistan Limited has adopted and applied the principles contained in the Code of Corporate Governance (COCG) in the following manner:

1) The Company encourages representation of independent non-executive directors. At present the Board includes five non-executive directors.

2) The resident directors have confirmed that none of them is serving as a director in more than ten listed companies, including this Company.

3) All the resident directors of the Company are registered as taxpayers and none of them have defaulted in payment of any loan to a banking company, a DFI or an NBFC or, being a member of a stock exchange, has been declared as a defaulter by that stock exchange.

4) No casual vacancy occurred during the year on the Board.

5) The Company has prepared a 'Statement of Ethics and Business Practices', which has been signed by all the directors and employees of the Company.

6) The Board has developed a vision/mission statement, overall corporate strategy, business conduct principles and significant policies of the Company. A complete

EXHIBIT 3 (CONTINUED)

CASES IN CORPORATE GOVERNANCE 59

record of particulars of significant policies along with the dates on which they were approved or amended has been maintained.

7) All the powers of the Board have been duly exercised and decisions on material transactions, including appointment and determination of remuneration and terms and conditions of employment of the CEO, have been taken by the Board.

8) The meetings of the Board were presided over by the Chairman, and the Board met at least once in every quarter. Written notices of the Board meetings, along with agenda and working papers, were circulated at least seven days before the meetings. The minutes of the meetings were appropriately recorded and circulated.

9) The directors have confirmed that they are well acquainted of their duties and responsibilities as required under the COCG. However, information material including a copy of the COCG and the Memorandum and Articles of Association of the Company were circulated to the directors to apprise them with their duties and responsibilities and enable them to manage the affairs of the Company.

10) The Board approves the appointment of CFO/Company Secretary and Head of Internal Audit, including their remuneration and terms and conditions of employment, as recommended by the CEO.

11) The directors' report for this year has been prepared in compliance with the requirements of the Code and fully describes the salient matters required to be disclosed.

12) The financial statements of the Company were duly endorsed by CEO and CFO before approval of the Board.

13) The directors, CEO, and executives do not hold any interest in the shares of the Company other than that disclosed in the pattern of shareholding.

14) The Company has complied with all the corporate and financial reporting requirements of the Code.

15) The Board has formed a Board Audit Committee, which comprises of three members, of whom two are non-executive directors.

16) The meetings of the Board Audit Committee were held at least once every quarter prior to approval of interim and final results of the Company and as required by the Code, the terms of reference of the Committee have been formed and advised to the Committee for compliance.

17) The Board has set-up an effective internal audit function.

18) The statutory auditors of the Company have confirmed that they have been given a satisfactory rating under the quality control review programme of the Institute of Chartered Accountants of Pakistan, that they or any of the partners of the firm, their spouses, and minor children do not hold shares of the Company and that the firm and all its partners are in compliance with International Federation of Accountants (IFAC) guidelines on code of ethics as adopted by the Institute of Chartered Accountants of Pakistan.

19) The statutory auditors or the persons associated with them have not been appointed to provide other services except in accordance with the listing regulations and the auditors have confirmed that they have observed IFAC guidelines in this regard.

20) We confirm that all other material principles contained in the Code have been complied with as stated above.

For and on behalf of the Board of Directors of

Karachi   NAIM FAROOQUI
26 September 2008   **Chief Executive**

Source: Company Annual Report 2008.

EXHIBIT 4

CASES IN CORPORATE GOVERNANCE   61

EXTRACTS FROM NOTES TO THE FINANCIAL STATEMENTS FOR THE HALF YEAR ENDED DECEMBER 2007

	Dec. 2007	June 2007
14. DEFICIT ON REVALUATION OF SECURITIES	Rupees in millions	
Available-for-sale financial assets		
Government securities	(63)	(63)
Quoted securities		
Ordinary shares	(457)	–
Term finance certificates–quoted	0	(4)
Units of open-ended mutual funds	44	44
	(412)	40
Sub-total–available-for-sale financial assets	**(475.89)**	**(22.89)**
Held for trading investments		
Quoted securities		
Ordinary shares	(27.88)	(10.6)
Units of closed-end mutual funds	(24.70)	(9)
	(52.58)	(19.6)
Fair value of derivative financial instruments	5	0.5
Sub-total–held for trading investments	(523.47)	(41.99)
Related deferred tax asset on government securities	22.16	16.48
Total deficit on revaluation of securities	**(501.31)**	**(25.51)**

Source: Company Annual Report.

KARACHI STOCK EXCHANGE SHARE PRICE QUOTATIONS

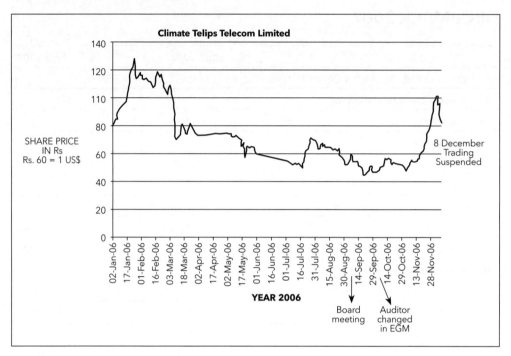

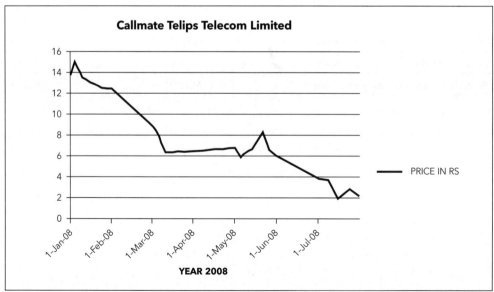

EXHIBIT 5 (CONTINUED)

CASES IN CORPORATE GOVERNANCE   63

KARACHI STOCK EXCHANGE SHARE PRICE QUOTATIONS (CONT.)

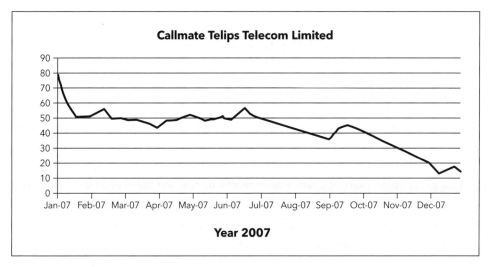

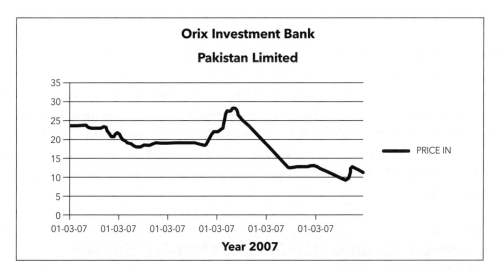

Source: Data from the Karachi Stock Exchange.

EXTRACTS FROM NOTES TO THE FINANCIAL STATEMENTS OF 2008

1. Status And Nature Of Business

1.1 ORIX Investment Bank Pakistan Limited ('the Company') was incorporated as a public limited company in Pakistan under the name of ORIX Investment Finance Company Pakistan Limited. Subsequently, the name of the Company was changed to ORIX Investment Bank Pakistan Limited. The registered office of the Company is situated at Overseas Investors Chamber of Commerce Building, Talpur Road, Karachi, Pakistan. The Company is licensed to carry out investment finance services as a Non-Banking Finance Company (NBFC) under the Non- Banking Finance Companies (Establishment and Regulations) Rules 2003, issued by the Securities and Exchange Commission of Pakistan (SECP) as amended by SRO 1131(1)/2007 of SECP dated 21 November 2007. The Company is listed on the Karachi and Lahore Stock Exchanges. The Company is a corporate member of the Karachi Stock Exchange (Guarantee) Limited and Lahore Stock Exchange (Guarantee) Limited and is also engaged in equity brokerage service.

1.2 The Company has incurred a net loss after tax amounting to Rs. 664.29 million during the year ended 30 June 2008 (2007: Loss after tax Rs. 311.97 million) and as of that date, its accumulated losses amount to Rs. 865.15 million (2007: accumulated losses Rs. 200.86 million). As a result, the Company is presently not meeting the minimum equity requirement of Rs. 500 million as specified by NBFC and Notified Entities Regulations, 2007. However, in view of financial support from ORIX Corporation—Japan and favourable financial projections, management is confident to come out from the current loss situation

4. Non-Compliance Of NBFC And Notified Entities Regulation, 2007

4.1 In accordance with regulation no. 3 of Non-Banking Finance Companies and Notified Entities Regulations 2007, an NBFC licensed by the commission to undertake business of investment finance services shall meet minimum equity requirements of Rs. 500 million

EXHIBIT 6 (CONTINUED)

CASES IN CORPORATE GOVERNANCE   65

as at 30 June 2008. However, the equity of the Company as at 30 June 2008 is Rs. 419.89 million (excluding the effect of deficit on revaluation of securities), which does not comply with the above-mentioned requirement.

4.2 In accordance with regulation no. 28 of Non-Banking Finance Companies and Notified Entities Regulation, 2007, 'An NBFC duly licensed to provide investment finance service shall not make total investment in shares, equities or scrips in excess of one hundred percent of its own equity and such NBFC shall not own shares, equities or scrips of any one company in excess of ten percent of its own equity or of the issued capital of the company, whichever is less.' However, the following does not comply with the above requirement:

1) The total investment (valued at cost) of the Company in shares, open ended and closed ended mutual funds as at 30 June 2008 is Rs. 604.36 million, while the equity of the Company is Rs. 419.89 million (excluding the effect of deficit on revaluation of securities).

2) The individual investments of the Company in certain shares as at 30 June 2008 exceed the above mentioned.

Source: Company Annual Report.

2008 REVIEW REPORT TO THE MEMBERS ON STATEMENT OF COMPLIANCE WITH BEST PRACTICES OF CODE OF CORPORATE GOVERNANCE

We have reviewed the Statement of Compliance with the best practices contained in the Code of Corporate Governance prepared by the Board of Directors of **ORIX Investment Bank Pakistan Limited** ("the Company") to comply with the Listing Regulation No. 37 of the Karachi Stock Exchange, Chapter XIII of the Listing Regulations of the Lahore Stock Exchange where the Company is listed.

The responsibility for compliance with the Code of Corporate Governance is that of the Board of Directors of the Company.

Our responsibility is to review—to the extent where such compliance can be objectively verified—whether the Statement of Compliance reflects the status of the Company's compliance with the provisions of the Code of Corporate Governance and report if it does not. A review is limited primarily to inquiries of the Company's personnel and review of various documents prepared by the Company to comply with the Code.

As part of our audit of financial statements we are required to obtain an understanding of the accounting and internal control systems sufficient to plan the audit and develop an effective audit approach. We have not carried out any special review of the internal control system to enable us to express an opinion as to whether the Board's statement on internal control covers all controls and the effectiveness of such internal controls.

Based on our review nothing has come to our attention, which causes us to believe that the Statement of Compliance does not appropriately reflect the Company's compliance, in all material respects, with the best practices contained in the Code of Corporate Governance as applicable to the Company for the year ended 30 June 2008.

Karachi   KPMG Taseer Hadi & Co.
26 September 2008   Chartered Accountants

Source: Company Annual Report 2008.

Copyright © 2016: One time permission to reproduce granted by Richard Ivey School of Business Foundation on 25 November 2016.

1.3 CRESCENT STANDARD INVESTMENT BANK LIMITED—GOVERNANCE FAILURE

CASE HIGHLIGHTS AND KEY POINTS

The Crescent Standard Investment Bank Limited (CSIBL) was the largest investment bank quoted on all the stock exchanges in Pakistan, so when it declared a huge loss of Rs. 2.1 billion (US$35.5 million) for the year ended 31 December 2005, the market was taken by surprise. There had been some rumours that all was not well and that the investment banking regulator, the Securities and Exchange Commission of Pakistan (SECP), had sent a team of officers to investigate the affairs of the bank. Since the main shareholders were individuals or companies of the well-known business group known as the Crescent Group, there was enormous interest in the CSIBL affairs by financial and political circles as well. The case describes the various types of entities that were merged to form the CSIBL, principally to protect the stakeholders by creating an entity with a large capitalization. The bank had reported in its annual reports that all the internal control mechanisms for good governance stipulated by the SECP were in place and the auditors (internal and external) had reported that these were satisfactory. Yet, when subjected to an investigation, it was revealed that the internal management was involved in a variety of acts of misrepresentation and concealment. The case focuses on the weaknesses in the structure of the corporate governance regime in Pakistan. The fact remains that no amount of internal or external checks can stop the internal management from colluding to perpetuate a fraud.

The Crescent Standard Investment Bank Limited (CSIBL) case has been developed from information available in the public domain. The case includes the details of the frauds committed within the investment bank and it focuses the students' attention to a number of elements that are essential for corporate governance to be effective. The students while going through this case can examine the following:

1. The ethical standards and responsibility of the Board of Directors with regard to day-to-day decisions especially regarding dealings with related companies.

2. The obligation and degree of due care and transparency of the operations of the Board is due to all the stakeholders in a public listed financial institution.

3. The reasons why the existing framework of controls based on code of corporate governance, internal audits, audit committees and the external audit was ineffective.

4. Could certain laws be enacted to prevent such cases on the pattern of Sarbanes Oxley Act 2002 in USA where the CEO and CFO face a stiff jail sentence if found guilty of a similar fraud? There were no restraints placed on the individual freedom of any of CSIBL directors- they were scot free.

Post-Enron legislation in the US in the form of the Sarbanes-Oxley Act 2002 affected businesses around the world. For public company financial executives, compliance with Section 404 of the Sarbanes-Oxley Act required disciplined project management and a thorough consideration of the appropriate roles to be played by management and its advisors and auditors.

POTENTIAL USES OF THE CASE

This case can be used in an MBA program to highlight a variety of issues in various courses:

1. Financial institutions or Islamic banking course:

   To examine the operation and management structure of non-bank financial institutions business areas including Islamic banking: modarabas, leasing, investment banking, and growth of an organization by mergers. There is financial data that can be used to show the measures of performance by conducting some financial analysis.

2. Ethics in a business course:

   A financial institution with the public as its shareholders raises the level of transparency required from its management. This case highlights how the performance of an organization is affected by the quality and standard of governance implemented by senior management. A suggestion can be made that the corporate laws be strengthened so that stiff penalties are imposed on rogue managers as a deterrent against deviant behavior.

3. Corporate law in a business course:

   Each of the different frauds can be evaluated as to whether it was a criminal act or a tort. The rules of the respective regulatory agencies can be examined to conduct a mock trial of the perpetrators of the fraud. Suggestions can be made to strengthen the law relating to public companies on the pattern of the Sarbanes-Oxley Act in the United States.

ASSIGNMENT QUESTIONS

1. What are the key controls that govern the supervision of a non-banking finance company listed on the Karachi Stock Exchange?

2. What were the reasons for the fraud and how could this event have been prevented?

3. Evaluate the statements made by the chairman and the director that in effect were avoiding any responsibility. What is the role of the board as a whole and the chairman in particular?

4. What was the effect of the mergers on the organization's culture?

5. Comment on the CSIBL internal management as indicated by the extracts of the annual reports and financial statements at 31 December 2004.

6. Prepare a report for the senior management of KET Securities recommending a course of action.

CASE TEXT: CRESCENT STANDARD INVESTMENT BANK LIMITED—GOVERNANCE FAILURE[1]

KET Securities Limited's head office at Karachi in Pakistan had been receiving unofficial reports since May 2006 that there had been a number of frauds at Crescent Standard Investment Bank Limited (CSIBL). This was confirmed when the bank did not circulate the audited accounts for the year ended 31 December 2005, even as late as August 2006. Early in September 2006, a business analyst at KET was asked to investigate what the press had been reporting. Management was shocked to read the information the newspapers had published (see Exhibit 1). He was to submit an analysis for senior management who had recently deposited some of the company funds as an investment in CSIBL, and he wondered what he should recommend.

CSIBL was part of the well-reputed Pakistani business conglomerate known as the Crescent Group and members of the group, individuals as well as companies, were also its majority shareholders. CSIBL had evolved after mergers of a number of financial institutions. It had commenced operating as CSIBL after the merger of First Standard Investment Bank

---

1   This case has been written on the basis of published sources only. Consequently, the interpretation and perspectives presented in this case are not necessarily those of Crescent Standard Investment Bank Limited or any of its employees.

Limited and First Crescent Modaraba in 2003. During 2004 and 2005, the business in the modaraba[2] sector had seen growth but it was facing stiff competition from commercial banks. While some gains were achieved on the stock market, the spread income was inadequate and kept profitability low. In 2005, after a period of four years, the federal government had constituted the Religious Board for the Modarabas. This was expected to help by allowing new avenues of business. In order to enhance the risk absorption capacity of the sector, acquisitions and voluntary mergers were being encouraged by the Security Exchange Commission of Pakistan (SECP). The series of mergers of various businesses was indicative of a general strategic shift towards consolidation that was needed to usher financial stability and operational flexibility (see Exhibit 2). In order to facilitate the operations of non-banking institutions, the SECP had first issued the prudential regulations for the non-banking finance companies (NBFCs) in early 2004 and these were amplified in 2006. These were also intended to help with improving the risk management and corporate governance of the modarabas (see Exhibit 3).

MERGERS AND ACQUISITIONS BY THE CRESCENT GROUP

The objective of the Crescent Group was to achieve growth by takeovers and mergers with other NBFCs. First Crescent Modaraba started acquisitions in 1999 and by 2003 had acquired two modarabas and merged with an investment bank. The various activities of the NBFCs were leasing, investment banking, housing finance, venture capital, discounting, asset management, and investment advisory services. With the aim of creating a level playing field for the banking and non-banking financial sector, the SECP and State Bank of Pakistan (SBP) had been introducing reforms. Since the NBFCs were not allowed retail deposit gathering, the ability to raise finance for the NBFCs was made easier by the SBP allowing the commercial banks to underwrite term finance certificates (TFCs), commercial papers, and other debt instruments issued by the NBFCs.

---

2   *Modaraba (profit-sharing)*: an arrangement or agreement between the bank, or a capital provider, and an entrepreneur, whereby the entrepreneur can mobilize the funds of the former for its business activity. The entrepreneur provides expertise, labor and management. Profits made are shared between the bank and the entrepreneur according to a predetermined ratio. In the case of loss, the bank loses the capital, while the entrepreneur loses his provision of labor. It is this financial risk, according to the Shariah, that justifies the bank's claim to part of the profit. The profit-sharing continues until the loan is repaid. The bank is compensated for the time value of its money in the form of a floating interest rate that is pegged to the debtor's profits.

As the operating environment was difficult, the Crescent Group was continuing its policy of growth by merger and acquisition. In Lahore on 6 August 2002, the shareholders in two listed entities—Altowfeek Investment Bank and First Crescent Modaraba—gave their approval to the scheme of arrangement for amalgamation of the two companies into 'First Standard Investment Bank Limited' (FSIBL). After the amalgamation, the Crescent Group held 35 per cent shares and was able to place three nominees on the seven-member board of First Standard Investment Bank Limited (see Exhibit 4). Altowfeek Bank had a paid in capital of Rs. 310 million which had been eroded by losses of around Rs. 275 million, so the merged entity had a paid in capital of Rs. 345 million (see Exhibit 6). The strategy of the Crescent Group appeared to have been to combine the modarabas, investment banks and the two leasing companies into a kind of financial supermarket.

KET knew the determination of the Crescent Group, as earlier in 23 July 2002, First Leasing Corporation Limited (FLCL) had informed the Karachi Stock Exchange that three nominee directors of Pak-Libya Holding Company had been replaced by nominees of the Crescent Group. The proceedings of the annual general meeting of FSIBL on Monday, 15 August (see Exhibit 5), confirmed the 23 July report. The Crescent Group had purchased the strategic equity interests held by Pak-Libya Holdings Limited in two leasing companies—First Leasing Corporation Limited and Paramount Leasing Company Limited (PLCL)—for a cash consideration of Rs. 175 million. The daily Dawn had reported that changes on the board of directors of Paramount were to be made at the meeting of its board scheduled for 27 August. Both publicly traded companies—First Leasing Corporation Limited and Paramount Leasing Company Limited—had earlier been in advanced talks for a merger, which would have created a new leasing company, 'First Paramount'. The Crescent Group was understood to have paid Rs. 5 per share to Pak-Libya for its 36 per cent stake in First Leasing, while acquiring the 56 per cent majority holding in Paramount Leasing at Rs. 10 per share. The group had intended to induct four nominees on the seven-member board of directors of Paramount on 27 August and thereby gain control (see Exhibit 5). When the proposed merger of Paramount with First Leasing was completed, the Crescent Group held 52 per cent equity in the merged company—First Paramount Leasing Company (FPLC).

Capital Adequacy

The paid-up capital of First Leasing was Rs. 272 million and that of Paramount Rs. 250

million, which made the combined capital of First Paramount Rs. 522 million—the largest among 32 companies listed on the leasing sector. Interestingly, over 80 per cent equity in both leasing companies was vested in financial institutions, which was why acquisition of a majority stake looked both an easier and timelier strategic move for the Crescent Group. According to a report of FSIBL to the Lahore Stock Exchange (LSE), the board of directors of FSIBL, in view of the decision of SECP, had approved 15 June 2004 as the effective date of the merger/amalgamation. The allotment of shares of FSIBL would be made on 25 June 2004, in exchange for shares of FLCL, PLCL, and FPLC. Things appeared to have progressed according to plan for the Crescent Group and the foundations were laid for CSIBL as the name of FSIBL (see Exhibit 6) was changed in 2004.

Merger Results

Crescent Standard Investment Bank Limited, formerly First Standard Investment Bank Limited (see Exhibit 7), had achieved a balance sheet footing of Rs. 9,407 million and a paid-up capital base of Rs. 1,258 million and adjusted equity stood at Rs. 2,054 million after all the mergers (the average rate in 2004 and 2005 was US$1=Rs. 58.50).

The financial results of CSIBL, after the mergers were completed, for the period of six months ended on 30 June 2004, showed:

1. Gross income, including lease revenue, of Rs. 186.63 million.

2. Return on finances, loans and placements of Rs. 121.96 million.

3. Return on investments of Rs. 179.43 million.

4. The financial charges had decreased substantially due to reduction in borrowings and markup rates; and

5. The company had earned after-tax profits of Rs. 205.13 million during the period under review as against after-tax losses of Rs. 88.87 million in the corresponding period.

During the period to 30 June 2004, the stock market had maintained a rising trend and the Karachi Stock Exchange KSE-100 index closed at 5,279 points on 30 June 2004, as against 4,472 points on 31 December 2003. This landmark performance of the stock market during the period could be attributed to a number of positive factors: pro-growth macro-economic policies and a stable macro-economic environment. The Bank had taken advantage of this rising trend in stock markets and earned capital gains and dividends of Rs. 138.959 million during the period to 30 June 2004. Management hoped that the cautious investment approach would reduce the market price fluctuation risks. The first half-yearly financial statements for the period of six months ended on 30 June 2004, after the merger showed that the company had become the largest investment bank in the country in terms of balance sheet size and equity base (see Exhibit 7).

Management of CSIBL

The operations of the merged entities remained at a low pace, constrained by the slow legal formalities of the merger process, which took a period of over one year. The synergies of the merger were expected to emerge in the coming periods. In the meantime, the company successfully completed management restructuring by consolidating the existing expertise available and also by hiring new professionals in order to provide the most efficient services to its customers. The chief executive officer (CEO) of the Bank had been with the Crescent Group earlier as CEO of First Crescent Modaraba since 1997. The CSIBL registered office was in Lahore and business was carried out through a network of four branches situated at the prime locations of Karachi, Lahore, Islamabad, and Peshawar. The new office building at Lahore, named as 'Crescent Standard Tower', was felt to be contributing towards the image-building of the company in the public at large.

The management stated that it was planning to further expand its business operations by opening eight new branches for broadening its customer base and intended to make the company one of the largest and most pioneering Islamic investment banks of the country. The management had inherited rich experience in Islamic investment banking (as a result of the merger with Altowfeek) and was also focusing on financing small and medium enterprises (SMEs) due to potential in these avenues. By 2006, CSIBL was engaged in a variety of activities:

1. Investment finance in accordance with the original license granted to FSIBL; and

2. Various other modes of funding and business, including leasing and Islamic financing.

The SECP supervised and regulated CSIBL operations under the Non-Banking Finance Companies (Establishment and Regulation) Rules 2003, and CSIBL shares were quoted on all the stock exchanges of Pakistan (see Exhibit 8).

CSIBL Declares Losses

In 2005, the Bank seemed to be progressing well, especially considering JCR-VIS Credit Rating Company Limited (JCR-VIS) had on 26 April 2005, upgraded the entity rating of CSIBL to 'BBB+/A-2' (Triple B Plus/A-Two) from 'BBB/A-3' (Triple B/A-Three), while the rating of CSIBL's outstanding TFC issue (formerly a liability of Pacific Leasing Corporation Limited) had also been upgraded to 'A-' (Single A Minus). The outlook on the medium- to long-term ratings was considered to be 'stable'.

The upgrade took into consideration all-around improvement in financial indicators. CSIBL's core profitability had improved and full profit retention had increased the level of capitalization. During the second half of the year ended December 2004, the focus of management had been towards consolidation of the institution. At the same time, the advances portfolio had shown substantial growth and greater emphasis had been made towards extending morabaha and musharika financing. The management had also undertaken an aggressive recovery drive against its delinquent portfolio. Nevertheless, CSIBL remained exposed to a degree of market risk on account of its equity holdings. In 2005, International Finance Corporation, the arm of the World Bank that lent to the private sector, had reposed confidence in CSIBL by extending a line of credit to finance SMEs (see Exhibit 9).

In July 2006, the press reported that CSIBL had defaulted in payment of the sixth redemption of term finance certificates (TFC) issue of Rs. 350 million. The TFC holders were due to receive Rs. 66 million as the third payment on 8 July 2006. A large holder of the TFC, Pak-Oman Investment Company Limited, started court proceedings against CSIBL and this shook the financial markets as it was the first ever default of a listed instrument in the country. This TFC was formerly a liability of Pacific Leasing Corporation Limited, which had been merged into CSIBL.

The market was taken by surprise when Crescent Standard Investment Bank reported negative earnings results for the year ended 31 December 2005. The accounts showed a huge loss of PKR 2.118 billion, which converted into a loss per share of Rs. 16.85, meaning the entire equity stood eroded and the book value was negative Rs. 6.85 per share.

The KET analyst felt that the sudden decline of performance could only have been due to an internal fraud, as the CSIBL appeared to have some of the main corporate governance controls in place, such as:

1. Regular board of directors meetings (see Exhibit 4);

2. An internal audit department and audit committee;

3. Unqualified external audit reports;

4. A statement of compliance with the Code of Corporate Governance; and

5. Good ratings by a credit rating agency.

He wanted to examine how this fraud had been carried out and was particularly concerned at the statements made by directors, including the chairman of CSIBL, who was also the full-time chief executive and shareholder of an associated company—International Housing Finance Limited (see Exhibit 10). The chairman and director of CSIBL, Manzurul Haq, had claimed in a press report that he was not informed and was ignorant while the parallel deals were being made. The relevant SECP excerpt read as follows:

> The Commission had also received a letter, dated 22 June 2006, from Manzur-ul-Haq, Chairman and Director of the Bank, which reads, in relevant parts, as under:
>
> Recent events, like the unearthing of the J O Vohra transaction [see Exhibit 11] and the sale of assets of the bank without the Board's prior approval or knowledge

bring me to the sad conclusion that the Board and its resolutions have no sanctity and the Board at best is irrelevant at the Bank.[3]

Another board director, Iftikhar Soomro, had noted that:

> After the commencement of inspection by SECP, the board, particularly independent directors, advised several remedial measures. However, we regret to note that the resolutions of the board were consistently bypassed and the board was rendered totally ineffective to exercise control over the affairs of the Bank. The ineffectiveness of the board members is largely attributable to the sponsors and their control over executive directors (management).[4]

As is the case in frauds, the business analyst knew that he had a monumental task, but he was determined that his report to KET management should be as incisive as the available facts would allow.

---

3   Business Recorder, 19 September 2006.

4   Ibid.

EXCERPTS FROM NEWS/PRESS REPORTS

Show-cause served on CEO of Crescent Standard Investment Bank

KARACHI (15 April 2006): A show-cause notice has been served on the Chief Executive Officer of Crescent Standard Investment Bank Limited (CSIBL) by the Securities and Exchange Commission of Pakistan (SECP) following discovery by its inspectors that the bank was 'maintaining parallel books of account' under the head of 'Managed Portfolio'.

During the inspection conducted in September last year, the SECP inspectors also found that while published accounts for the half year ended 30 June 2005 showed an asset base of Rs. 9.5529 billion, the parallel balance sheet showed an asset footing of Rs. 5.252 billion.

Along with the show-cause notice, which was issued on 17 March, the SECP in a separate letter issued on the same date restrained the CSIBL from extending financial facilities to its holding, subsidiary or associated companies, including such other companies as may become associated hereafter.

The inspectors found that the bank had entered into a number of transactions in violation of various provisions of the Companies Ordinance, 1984, especially sections 230 and 234 of the Ordinance and Rule 7(1) (a) of Non-Banking Finance Companies (NBFC) Rules.

The parallel books of account showed a placement of an amount of Rs. 1.817 billion in investment made by the bank in 20.896 million shares of PICIC-DFI [Pakistan Industrial Credit Investment Finance Corporation].

Investments were made through borrowing from various financial institutions as well as general public. This fact and amount of liabilities were, however, excluded from the books of accounts of the bank as on 31 December 2004 and 30 June 2005 despite the fact that it represents a liability of the bank. The books of accounts of the bank, therefore, failed to give a true and fair view of the affairs of the bank during that period.

The show-cause notice points out that the bank was maintaining six accounts in the name

EXHIBIT 1 (CONTINUED)

CASES IN CORPORATE GOVERNANCE   79

of Jhang Electric Supply Corporation (JESCO), depicting an aggregate activity of Rs. 5.918 billion over a period of time. These accounts were not reported in the printed general ledger of the said branch as of 30 June 2005.

Besides several other violations which had been listed in the show-cause notice, the bank entered into Musharaka[5] venture with its associate company Maghrib Development Corporation (Pvt) Ltd (MDPL) for an amount of Rs. 1.540 billion, out of which Rs. 655 million are shown in published accounts and Rs. 885 million are in parallel books of accounts maintained by the bank as double account. The show-cause notice also took cognisance of section 282-C of the ordinance whereby the CSBIL entered into Musharaka transactions with MDPL of Rs. 1.540 billion for investment in real estate. The bank did not possess a housing finance license as is required for this business and is, therefore, in violation of the section.

It also refers to the violation by the bank of the Prudential Regulations (PR) issued by the SECP under Section 282-D of the ordinance. The show-cause notice said: 'It is evident from the proceedings that you, in your capacity as the CEO of the bank have mismanaged the affairs of the bank and have willfully made statements which are false and omitted to make material statements.'

The SECP notice highlighted the use of bank assets to illegally benefit Anjum Saleem and Altaf Saleem. The details run as under: 'It has come to the knowledge of the commission that the bank has paid Rs. 50 million each on behalf of Altaf Saleem, sponsor of Crescent Group and Anjum Saleem, sponsor and chief executive of the bank.'

This matter was taken up with the bank. The commission undertook a targeted inspection from 27 to 30 June 2006 in this regard. This inspection resulted in a report (the third inspection report), wherein it was found as follows:

The examination of relevant records/books of accounts pertaining to the payment of

---

5   Musharika, or sharika, meaning partnership, is an Islamic mode of finance in which capital is provided by two or more parties for project development. Banks can participate in equity along with the project sponsors. The profits are shared among the parties on the basis of their participation or on a pre-agreed ratio and the losses are shared on the basis of equity participation. The difference between musharika and mudaraba is that in musharika, all involved parties provide capital to share in the profit or loss of the project. In mudaraba, one party provides the capital and the other acts as an agent to invest it. The agent in a mudaraba does not share in the losses.

EXHIBIT 1 (CONTINUED)

Rs. 100 million by the CSIBL to Habib Bank Ltd, KSE branch, Karachi on 27 April 2006 revealed that during the month of February 2005, two running finance facilities of Rs. 50 million each were offered by Habib Bank Ltd, KSE branch, Karachi to Altaf Saleem and Anjum Saleem.

The said facilities were granted for the period of one year expiring on 31 January 2006 and the purpose of the facilities was trading in stocks. The offer letters to this effect were issued by the chief manager, Habib Bank Ltd, KSE branch, Karachi to Altaf Saleem and Anjum Saleem on 9 February 2005 and 28 February 2005, respectively.

The facility of Rs. 50 million each was granted by the Habib Bank Ltd to Altaf Saleem and Anjum Saleem against a pledge of the following equity portfolio of the CSIBL, PICIC, SNGPL, PIA, Pakistan PTA, General Tyres, and SSGC. Anjum Saleem availed the running facility of Rs. 50 million from Habib Bank Ltd, KSE branch, Karachi by drawing a cheque dated 8 April 2005 for payment to the CSIBL.

The SECP now appointed A. Ferguson and Company, chartered accountants, to look into the affairs of the bank and submit the report, which is being compiled and is expected to be submitted to the SECP on 20 April.

In the other letter to Manzur-ul-Haq, Chairman, Board of Directors, Anjum Saleem and Iftikhar Soomro, Directors, that in view of the violations, the SECP, in exercise of its powers under Section 282-D of the Companies Ordinance 1984, has directed the bank to cease financial facilities to its holding, subsidiary, or associated companies which include the following:

Shakarganj Mills Limited, Crescent Leasing Corporation Limited, Crescent Standard Modarba, Safeway Mutual Funds Limited, Asian Stock Funds Limited, International Housing Finance Limited [see Exhibit 8], Crescent Commercial Bank Limited, PICIC Commercial Bank Limited, Pakistan Industrial Credit & Investment Corporation Limited, Crescent Business Management (Pvt) Limited, Maghrib Development Corporation (Pvt) Limited, Crescent Standard Aviation (Pvt) Limited, Crescent Brokerage & Investment Services Limited, Crescent Capital Management (Pvt) Limited, Crescent Standard Business Management (Pvt) Limited, Crescent Ujala Limited, Crescent Standard Telecommunications Limited, Crescent Steel & Allied Products Limited, Crescent

EXHIBIT 1 (CONTINUED)

CASES IN CORPORATE GOVERNANCE   81

Modaraba Management Company Limited, Altern Energy Limited, Crescent Bahuman Energy Limited, Crescent Bahuman Limited, Crescent Sugar Mills & Distillery Limited, Crescent Textile Mills Limited, Crescent Knitwear Limited, Crescent Industrial Chemicals Limited, Crescent Group Engineering (Pvt) Limited, and Crescent Jute Products Limited.

Source: *Business Recorder*, 15 April 2006.

CSIBL Case: Government keen to refer matter to house committee, National Assembly told.

ISLAMABAD (7 September 2006): Conceding gross financial bungling in the Crescent Standard Investment Bank, the government in National Assembly on Wednesday showed keenness for referring the matter to House standing committee, when the opposition members raised it through a call-attention notice.

The Parliamentary Affairs Minister, Sher Afgan Niazi acknowledged that the notice was absolutely on merit, and the government would like the people responsible to be punished. He read out a detailed 'charge-sheet' against the concerned bank, prepared by Finance Division, and said that State Minister for Finance Omar Ayub was to handle the issue. But the latter was not available at that time.

The bank, with which the name of Chairman of Earthquake Rehabilitation and Reconstruction (Erra) [a government relief organization] Altaf Saleem was being allegedly attached, he said, had Rs. 643 million negative equity that was detected through a special audit last year.

Speaker Amir Hussain agreeing to the opposition's demand, also called for thorough investigation. However, he did not say anything about the proposal on formation of a House committee to separately look into the issue.

When the mover, Sherry Rehman, Ghulam Murtaza Satti, Naveed Qamar, Ejaz Jakhrani, and Zulfiqar Gondol called for removal of the Erra chief for allegedly having direct involvement in the irregularities, the Minister said that recommendations of the committee would be implemented and action would be taken after responsibility is fixed.

EXHIBIT 1 (CONTINUED)

The Minister said that Erra funds were not at the disposal of Altaf Saleem. Therefore, there was no question of embezzlement. Likewise, the Auditor-General and some foreign donors would also be making sure that funds are justifiably disposed of, he added.

The Minister noted that the bank was involved in violation of the regulatory framework. In the light of the SECP's findings, the Board members were suspended and the bank's chief executive officer was removed.

Special audit was initiated and A. F. Ferguson-Chartered Accountants was appointed to review the assets and liabilities of the bank as on 31 October and 31 December 2005, which showed Rs. 13.62 billion asset base and Rs. 643 million negative equity.

He said that show-cause notices were issued to Mahmood Ahmad, ex-chief executive of the bank, to the board of directors, Shahid Latif Dar, ex-CFO, to the statutory auditors Syed Hussain & Co, Chartered Accountants.

Likewise, a show-cause notice was issued for cancellation of its leasing and investment finance licences and moving of winding up petition. Another show-cause notice under section 282-F read with sub-section (1) and the proviso to sub-section (2) of section 282-E of the Companies Ordinance, 1984 was issued.

The Minister made it clear that no special 'cows' or 'bulls' were being created, when opposition members charged that the government was protecting the Erra chairman.

He assured that the responsible people would be punished under the Companies Act, and proposed that the committee should conclude its findings within the stipulated time.

Source: *Business Recorder*, 7 September 2006.

EXHIBIT 2

CASES IN CORPORATE GOVERNANCE   83

LIST OF COMPANIES FORMING THE CSIBL

No.	Name of Company	New name of the company/merged with	Date of Merger	Paid-up Capital (RS millions)	Ratio
1	Al Ata Leasing Modaraba	First Crescent Modaraba	03-Dec-1999	57.750	[1:2.905]
2	1st Confidence Modaraba	First Crescent Modaraba	23-Feb-2001	60.500	[0.93]
3	First Crescent Modaraba	AlTowfeek Investment Bank	06-Aug-2002	345.000	[1.53:1]
4	First Crescent Modaraba	First Standard Investment Bank Ltd.	31-July-2003	226.187	[1:3]
5*	Paramount Leasing Limited	First Standard Investment Bank Limited	06-June-2004	250.000	[0.513:1]
6*	First Leasing Corporation Limited	First Standard Investment Bank Limited	06-June-2004	272.783	[3.268:1]
7*	Pacific Leasing Company Limited	First Standard Investment Bank Limited	06-June-2004	200.000	[0.555:1]

* Details are given below.

Source: Karachi Stock Exchange.

Scheme of the mergers of the three leasing companies:
According to the arrangement, one fully paid share of par value of Rs. 10 each of FSIBL would be issued against 0.513 ordinary shares of Rs. 10/-each of PLL, 0.555 ordinary shares of Rs. 10/-each of PLCL, and 3.268 ordinary shares of Rs. 10/- each of FLCL.

The assets and liabilities of the merging entities are adjusted to conform to the uniformity of the accounting policies of the combining enterprises and apply to all periods presented.

The merger was accounted for by recording assets (Rs. 3,807 million) and liabilities (Rs. 3,227 million) of the merging entities on effective dates as per schemes of arrangement, as under:

EXHIBIT 2 (CONTINUED)

1. Pacific Leasing (Assets: Rs. 859 million; Liabilities: Rs. 611 million);

2. Paramount Leasing (Assets: Rs. 2,499 million; Liabilities: Rs. 2,167 million);

3. First Leasing (Assets: Rs. 449 million; Liabilities: Rs. 449 million).

CSIBL had issued its 51.989 million ordinary shares to the shareholders of the merging entities as under:

1. Pacific Leasing—19.820 million shares (Swap Ratio: 0.555);

2. Paramount Leasing—26.803 million shares (Swap Ratio: 0.513);

3. First Leasing—5.366 million shares (Swap Ratio: 3.268).

The CEO of the various companies at the time of the merger:

No.	Name of Company	New name of the company/ merged with	CEO of the new company/ merged with
1	Al Ata Leasing Modaraba	First Crescent Modaraba	Mahmood Ahmad
2	1st Confidence Modaraba	First Crescent Modaraba	Mahmood Ahmad
3	First Crescent Modaraba	AlTowfeek Investment Bank	Mahmood Ahmad
4	First Crescent Modaraba	First Standard Investment Bank Limited	Mahmood Ahmad
5*	Paramount Leasing Limited	First Standard Investment Bank Limited	Mahmood Ahmad
6*	First Leasing Corporation Limited	First Standard Investment Bank Limited	Mahmood Ahmad
7*	Pacific Leasing Company Limited	First Standard Investment Bank Limited	Mahmood Ahmad

Source: Company Annual Reports.

EXHIBIT 3

CASES IN CORPORATE GOVERNANCE   85

EXCERPTS FROM NEWS/PRESS REPORTS

Prudential regulations for NBFCs announced: Consumer finance

ISLAMABAD, Jan. 9: The Securities and Exchange Commission of Pakistan (SECP) on Monday issued prudential regulations for consumer finance by non-banking finance companies (NBFCs). These will come into force with immediate effect.

The aim of the new regulations is to provide new avenues to investment banks, leasing companies, housing finance companies, and discount houses in order to enhance diversification and broaden their products range. The regulations include comprehensive operational guidelines and various risk management measures that have to be adopted by the NBFCs while initiating consumer financing.

Under the regulations, the board of directors of NBFCs is required to establish policies, procedures, and practices to define risks, stipulate responsibilities, specify security requirements, design internal controls, and then ensure strict compliance with them.

Pre-Operations:

Before embarking upon or undertaking consumer financing, the NBFCs will implement the following guidelines:

The NBFCs shall establish separate risk management function for the purpose of consumer financing, which will be suitably staffed by personnel having sufficient expertise and experience in the field of consumer finance and business.

These companies shall prepare comprehensive consumer credit policy duly approved by their board of directors, which shall besides other things, cover loan administration, including documentation, disbursement, and appropriate monitoring mechanism.

The policy shall explicitly specify the functions, responsibilities, and various staff positions powers/authority relating to approval/sanction of consumer financing facility.

For every type of consumer finance activity, the NBFCs shall develop a specific programme. The programme shall include the objective and quantitative parameters for the eligibility of the borrower and determining the maximum permissible limit per borrower.

The NBFCs shall put in place an efficient computer-based management information system (MIS) for the purpose of consumer finance, which should be able to effectively cater to the needs of consumer financing portfolio and should be flexible enough to generate necessary information reports used by the management for effective monitoring of NBFCs' exposure in this segment.

Reports interrelating delinquencies with various types of customers or various attributes of the customers will enable the management to take important policy decisions and make appropriate modifications in the lending programme.

Quarterly product-wise profit and loss account will be duly adjusted with the provisions on account of classified accounts. These profit and loss statements should be placed before the board of directors in the immediate next board meeting. The branches of foreign banks in order to comply with this condition shall place the reports before a committee comprising of CEO/country manager, CFO, and head of consumer business.

The NBFCs shall develop comprehensive recovery procedures for the delinquent consumer loans. The recovery procedures may vary from product to product. However, distinct and objective triggers should be prescribed for taking pre-planned enforcement recovery measures.

The NBFCs desirous of undertaking consumer finance will become a member of at least one Consumer Credit Information Bureau. Moreover, the NBFCs may share information/data among themselves or subscribe to other databases as they deem fit and appropriate.

The NBFCs starting consumer financing are encouraged to impart sufficient training on an ongoing basis to their staff to raise their capability regarding various aspects of consumer finance.

EXHIBIT 3 (CONTINUED)

CASES IN CORPORATE GOVERNANCE   87

The NBFCs shall prepare standardized set of borrowing and recourse documents (duly cleared by their legal counsels) for each type of consumer financing.

Operations:

Consumer financing, like other credit facilities, must be subject to the NBFCs risk management process for this particular business. The process may include, identifying source of repayment and assessing customers ability to repay, his/her past dealings with an NBFC, the net worth and information obtained from a Consumer Credit Information Bureau.

At the time of granting facility under various modes of consumer financing, the NBFCs shall obtain a written declaration from the borrower divulging details of various facilities already obtained from other NBFCs. The NBFCs should carefully study the details given in the statement and allow fresh finance/limit only after ensuring that the total exposure in relation to the repayment capacity of the customer does not exceed the reasonable limits as laid down in the approved policies of the NBFC. The declaration will also help NBFCs to avoid exposure against a person having multiple facilities from different financial institutions on the strength of an individual source of repayment.

Before allowing any facility, the NBFCs shall preferably obtain credit report from the Consumer Credit Information Bureau of which they are a member. The report will be given due weightage while making credit decision.

Internal audit and control function of the NBFC, apart from other things, should be designed and strengthened so that it can efficiently undertake an objective review of the consumer finance portfolio from time to time to assess various risks and possible weaknesses. The internal audit should also assess the adequacy of the internal controls and ensure that the required policies and standards are developed and practiced. Internal audit should also comment on the steps taken by the management to rectify the weaknesses pointed out by them in their previous reports for reducing the level of risk.

The NBFCs shall ensure that any repayment made by the borrower is accounted for before applying mark-up on the outstanding amount.

Source: SECP.

EXTRACTS OF THE FIRST STANDARD INVESTMENT BANK ANNUAL GENERAL MEETINGS

(Financial Statements are in Exhibit 6)

The Annual Report for 2002 listed the seven directors on the Board and senior management as follows:

DIRECTORS

1.	Mr Shezi Nackvi	Nominee AlBaraka Investment & Development co. Jeddah
2.	Mr Iftikhar Soomro	Nominee AlBaraka Investment & Development co. Jeddah
3.	Mr Waleed A. G. Addas	Nominee Islamic Investment Bank. Jeddah
4.	Mr Hassan Aziz Bilgrami	Nominee National Investment Trust
5.	Mr Manzurul Haq	
6.	Dr Wasim Azhar	
7.	Mr Tariq Aleem	

CHIEF EXECUTIVE OFFICER   Mr Mahmood Ahmad

There were various changes in the members of the Board and there were eight meetings held during the eighteen month period 1 July 2001 to 31 December 2002 and were attended as follows:

Directors' Name	Appointed (Resigned)	No of Meetings In Tenor	Attended
Mr Khalid M Bhaimia	(02-09-2002)	6	4
Mr Khalid Majid	(15-02-2002 resigned as CEO)	3	3
Mr Osman A Suleiman	(15-02-2002)	3	2
Mr Iftikhar A Soomro		8	6
Mr Yelsin Oner	(15-02-2002)	3	nil
Dr Omer Zuhair Hafiz		8	nil
Mr Shezi Neckvi	02-09-2002	2	nil

EXHIBIT 4 (CONTINUED)

CASES IN CORPORATE GOVERNANCE 89

Mr Hassan Aziz Bilgrami	07-08-2001	8	7
Dr Wasim Azhar	15-02-2002	6	2
Mr Mahmood Ahmad	15-02-2002 appointed CEO	6	6
Mr Muhammd Awais Qureshi	15-02-2002	6	5
Mr Tariq Aleem	15-02-2002	6	6

[Case writer note: Mr Waleed A. J. Addas and Mr Manzurul Haq are not mentioned as having attended any meeting]

A comparison with the next year 2003 is as follows:

BOARD OF DIRECTORS

The Annual Report for 2003 listed the seven directors on the Board and senior management as follows:

DIRECTORS

1. Mr Shezi Nackvi   Nominee AlBaraka Investment & Development co. Jeddah
2. Mr Iftikhar Soomro   Nominee AlBaraka Investment & Development co. Jeddah
3. Mr Waleed A. J Addas   Nominee Islamic Investment Bank. Jeddah
4. Mr Hassan Aziz Bilgrami Nominee National Investment Trust
5. Mr Manzurul Haq   Chairman
6. Dr Wasim Azhar
7. Mr Tariq Aleem

CHIEF EXECUTIVE OFFICER   Mr Mahmood Ahmad

There were various changes in the members of the Board and there were five meetings held during the year 1 January 2003 to 31 December 2003 and were attended as follows:

Directors' Name	Appointed (Resigned)	No of Meetings In Tenor	Attended
Mr Hassan Aziz Bilgrami		5	5
Mr Iftikhar A Soomro		5	4
Mr Mahmood Ahmad		5	5
Mr Manzurul Haq	22-09-2003	2	2
Mr Muhammd Awais Qureshi	(22-09-2003)	3	1
Dr Omer Zuhair Hafiz	(22-09-2003)	3	nil
Mr Shezi Neckvi		5	nil
Mr Tariq Aleem		5	5
Dr Wasim Azhar		5	1
Mr Waleed A. J. Addas	22-09-2003	2	nil

The Notice to the AGM for 2003 included the following:

1. Special Business
To consider and if thought fit, to pass the following special resolution with or without modifications:

Resolved
That the change of name of the company from First Standard Investment Bank Limited to Crescent Investment Bank Limited, as proposed by the Board of Directors be and is hereby approved for sanction by Securities and Exchange Commission of Pakistan.

2. Explanatory Statement Required under Section 160(1) (b) of the Companies Ordinance 1984 in respect of the special business proposed to be approved by the shareholders

First Standard Investment Bank Limited (FSIBL) was established by amalgamation of First Crescent Modaraba (FCM) and Altowfeek Investment Bank Limited (ATIBL). In merged FSIBL, the equity stake of FCM certificate holders is 77.49 per cent whereas ATIBL shareholders equity stake is 22.51 per cent. The proposed change of name is being brought about to reflect the stake of the sponsors and Group's identity.

EXHIBIT 4 (CONTINUED)

CASES IN CORPORATE GOVERNANCE 91

The Directors of FSIBL, have no interest in the above said special resolution.

The Directors Report and Chief Executives Review to the Shareholders stated:

> In May 2003, by the Grace of God the Honorable Lahore High Court sanctioned the Scheme of arrangement for the merger of First Crescent Modaraba into First Standard Investment Bank Limited (FSIBL), almost after a period of one year from the date of our application. This caused delay in finalization of the financial reporting of the merged results of the two organizations. To effectively cater to the situation and to bring harmony of the financial reporting with the financial sector of the country, the company has adopted the calendar year as its financial year. Therefore the first financial statements after the merger covered a period of eighteen months of operations of the merged entity.

The review also stated:

> The management is pleased to inform you that your company took over the active management of Paramount Leasing Limited(PLL), Pacific Leasing Company Limited (PLCL) and First Leasing.

> Corporation Limited (FLCL) with a view to merging the companies with and into FSIBL in order to form a broad based investment bank with strong equity structure. Insha Allah by consolidating the above mentioned companies we will be achieving a balance sheet footing of around Rs. 6,500 million and a paid up capital of around Rs. 1,000 million that will be providing a much larger source of funds for investing on better investment avenues.

Source: Company Annual Report.

EXTRACTS FROM PARAMOUNT LEASING LIMITED ANNUAL REPORT 2003

BOARD OF DIRECTORS

Mr Mahmood Ahmad—Chairman	Nominee, Crescent Business Management (Pvt.) Limited[6]
Mr NasirAyub—Chief Executive	Nominee, Crescent Business Management (Pvt.) Limited
Mr Farooq Lakhani	Nominee, Crescent Business Management (Pvt.) Limited
Mr Wasif Mustafa Khan	Nominee, Crescent Business Management (Pvt.) Limited
Mr Tariq Aleem	Nominee, Crescent Business Management (Pvt.) Limited
Mr Shahid Latif Dar	Nominee, Crescent Business Management (Pvt.) Limited
Mr S.M. Yusuf	Nominee, Crescent Business Management (Pvt.) Limited

Chief Executive's Review

The Directors of the company endorse the accompanying Chief Executive's review on the performance of the company during the year and its future outlook.

Corporate Governance

Paramount Leasing Limited conducts its business in a responsible manner with honesty and integrity. We also have the same expectations from all those with whom we have relationships. We insist that all transactions be open and transparent.

---

6   Crescent Business Management (Pvt) Limited was a wholly-owned subsidiary of the Crescent Group.

EXHIBIT 5 (CONTINUED)

CASES IN CORPORATE GOVERNANCE   93

Paramount Leasing Limited does not use gratification as an instrument of any business or financial gain and employees are not authorized to give or receive any gift or payment, which may be construed as such. Employees are required to avoid personal activities or financial interests which conflict with responsibility to the Company. All transactions must comply with the laws and must be fairly and accurately reflected in the accounts.

The Directors of the company have reviewed the Code of Corporate Governance and are pleased to confirm that the company has made the compliance of the provisions set out by the Securities and Exchange Commission of Pakistan (SECP) and there is no material departure from the best practices as detailed in the listing regulations.

In the financial statements under review, we declare that:

-   The financial statements of the company represent the true and fair view of the Company's operations, cash flows and changes in equity. Proper books of the accounts of the company have been maintained.

-   Appropriate accounting policies have been consistently applied in preparation of financial statements except for the changes explained in financial statement and accounting estimates are based on reasonable and prudent judgment.

-   International Accounting Standard, as applicable in Pakistan has been followed in preparation of financial statements and any departure there from (if any) has been adequately disclosed.

-   Adequate system of international control is designed and being effectively implemented and mentioned by the management. There are no significant doubts upon the company's ability to continue as a going concern.

-   There has been no material departure from the best practices from the corporate governance, applicable at 30 June 2003. There has been no trading during the year in the shares of the company carried out by the directors, CEO, CFO, Company Secretary and their spouses and minor children.

Source: Paramount Leasing Limited Annual Report.

EXHIBIT 6

FIRST STANDARD INVESTMENT BANK FINANCIAL STATEMENT

Average exchange rate USD 1 = PKR 58.5		Rupees in Millions	
Performance Statistics	**12 Months to**	**18 Months to**	
Balance Sheet as at	**31/12/2003**	**31/12/2002**	**30/06/2001**
Share Capital-Paid-up:	738	738	536
Capital Reserves:	70	68	66
Accumulated (Loss):	(462)	(468)	(202)
Shareholders' Equity:	**345**	**338**	**401**
Surplus (Deficit) on Revaluation of Investments:	99	(13)	7
Supplementary Capital:	43	22	
Redeemable Capital:	277	528	795
L.T Deposits:	56	41	65
Customers Deposits:	614	152	5
Current Liabilities:	3,362	2,399	1,581
Total Liabilities & Equity	**4,797**	**3,467**	**2,855**
Tangible Fixed Assets:	758	674	709
Business Acquisitions:	281	298	0
Deposits, Deferred Cost & Asset:	121	121	42
Finances Under Morabaha Arrangements:	113	1	64
Long Term Investments:	180	350	546
Current Assets:	3,343	2,024	1,494
Total Assets:	**4,797**	**3,467**	**2,855**

	Rupees in Millions		
Performance Statistics			
	31/12/2003	**31/12/2002**	**30/06/2001**
Revenue, Profit & Pay Out	**12 months**	**18 Months**	**12 months**
Revenues			
Operating Lease Rentals	231	367	333

EXHIBIT 6 (CONTINUED)

CASES IN CORPORATE GOVERNANCE   95

Profit on Finances Under Musharaka/Morabah Arrangements:	85	200	223
Profits on Funds Placed With Financial Institutions:	23	58	5
Return on Investments:	216	59	5
Other Income:	34	24	51
Total Revenue	**589**	**708**	**617**
Financial charges:	377	515	320
Depreciation:	163	221	272
Administrative & other expenses:	42	60	48
Total Expenditures	**582**	**796**	**640**
PROFIT (LOSS) BEFORE PROVISIONS	7	(88)	(23)
Provisions:	5	(2)	(13)
Profit/(Loss) Before Taxation:	12	(90)	(36)
Taxation:	(6)	72	(16)
Profit/(Loss) After Tax	**6**	**(18)**	**(51)**
Earnings Per Share (Rs):	0.09	(0.25)	(0.70)

Source: First Standard Investment Bank Annual Report.

CRESCENT STANDARD INVESTMENT BANK LIMITED FINANCIAL STATEMENT

Performance Statistics	Rupees in millions	
Balance Sheet as at	31 Dec 2004	31 Dec 2003
Net Investment in Finance Lease:	2,512	2,834
Lending to Financial Institutions:	1,302	717
Investments:	1,435	950
Musharakah, etc:	2,219	778
Operating Fixed Assets:	750	250
Other assets:	1,190	1,134
Total Assets:	**9,407**	**6,663**
Redeemable Capital:	638	786
Security Deposits:	567	588
Customers Deposits:	3,870	1,863
Borrowings:	1,782	2,022
Other liabilities:	496	681
Total Liabilities:	**7,353**	**5940**
Net Assets:	**2,054**	**723**
Share Capital:	1,258	1,258
Reserves:	307	(577)
Surplus on Revaluation of Assets-Net of Tax:	423	0
Supplementary Capital:	67	43
Total Equity:	**2,054**	**723**
Contingency and Commitments:	622	371
Income Statement for	**Year to 31 Dec 2004**	**Year To 31 Dec 2003**
Lease Revenue:	307	342
Return on Finances and Placements:	478	177
Return on Investments:	298	240
Other income:	45	58

The accounts for year ended 31 December 2004 reflected the combined results of the merging entities on a uniting of interests basis in accordance with IAS No 22, "Business Combinations," by eliminating all inter-company transactions.

EXHIBIT 7 (CONTINUED)

CASES IN CORPORATE GOVERNANCE   97

Total Income:	**1,128**	**817**
Financial Charges:	457	638
Admin., and Operating Expenses:	185	166
Total Expenses	**642**	**804**
Profit Before Adjustments:	486	13
Provision for doubtful debts:	(7)	(110)
Adjustment for Trading investment:	(8)	
Profit (Loss) Before Taxation:	471	(96)
Taxation:	(11)	(14)
Profit (Loss) After Taxation:	**460**	**(110)**
Earnings/(Loss) Per Share Rs:	3.66	(0.87)

Source: Crescent Standard Investment Bank Annual Report.

EXHIBIT 8

SUMMARY OF MOVEMENT OF SHARE PRICES ON THE KARACHI STOCK EXCHANGE

Between Jul 07, 2004 and its last trade date, CSIBL achieved its highest closing price on Apr 21, 2005 (Rs. 18.40), and its lowest closing price on Sep 19, 2006 (Rs. 2.50). In intraday trading, it reached its highest price on Mar 17, 2005 (Rs. 19.40) and its lowest price on Sep 20, 2006 (Rs. 2.25).

The company's financial year end is 31 December each year. In the absence of any annual report after 2005, if the Annual Report of 2005 was used, which showed a huge loss and the closing price of Rs. 4.15 on 3 April 2007, CSIBL's ratios were all negative; book value was Rs. 5.12, its [Earnings Per Share] EPS was Rs. 16.85, and other ratios also did not make sense as the company's net worth was negative Rs. 643.40 million.

Company	Date	Open Rs.	Close Rs	Change Rs	High Rs.	Low Rs.	Volume of trades
CSIBL	Opening day 18 Nov 2004	9.80	9.80	–	–	–	Nil
	18 Feb 2005	16.50	16.40	–0.10	17.00	16.30	51,500
	4 April 2005	15.00	16.50	1.50	16.50	16.00	36,500
	30 June 2005		15.00	.00	.00	.00	None
	15 July 2005		16.50	.00	16.50	16.40	25,000
	14 Sept 2005		12.80	.80	12.90	12.10	668,500
	30 Dec 2005		12.10	.10	12.30	12.00	132,500
	29 Jan 2006		11.90	0.10	12.00	11.80	24,500
	17 Feb 2006		11.40	0.20	11.50	11.00	60,000
	No prices quoted						
	23 August 2006		4.10	–.40	4.40	4.10	35,000
	24 Sep 2006		2.80	0.00	3.10	2.80	380,000
	13 October 2006		5.50	0.30	5.75	4.45	3,788,000
	14 Nov 2006		4.45	.15	4.45	4.25	193,500
	No prices quoted						

EXHIBIT 8 (CONTINUED)

CASES IN CORPORATE GOVERNANCE   99

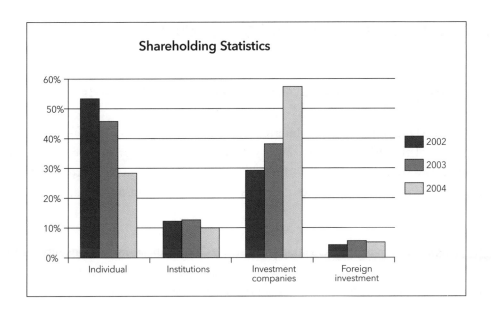

Source: Karachi and Lahore Stock Exchanges.

EXCERPT FROM NEWS/PRESS REPORT

7 million IFC loan for Crescent Bank to serve SMEs

ISLAMABAD (21 July 2005): The International Finance Corporation (IFC)—the private sector arm of the World Bank Group—will provide a loan of $7 million to Crescent Standard Investment Bank Ltd, to finance leasing of equipment to micro, small, and medium enterprises in agribusiness, services, construction, transportation, textile, and other sectors.

The loan facility is part of IFC's strategy to strengthen financial institutions serving the small enterprise sectors in Pakistan. These businesses are key drivers of economic growth in the country yet remain under-served by the formal financial sector.

Jyrki Koskelo, IFC's Director for Global Financial Markets, said, 'IFC is keen to help Pakistan's financial sector develop alternative sources of funding and expand into lending to new business sectors. We are pleased to be working with Crescent Standard Investment Bank to provide funding with longer maturities for its lending to micro and small businesses.'

'Smaller-scale enterprises are essential to economic growth and in Pakistan the leasing sector has significant potential to help develop such businesses,' Michael Essex, IFC's Associate Director for the Middle East and North Africa, said.

Mahmood Ahmed, Chief Executive Officer of Crescent Standard Investment Bank Limited, said, 'We are pleased that IFC has provided us with funding on a long-term basis and in a very timely fashion. This transaction will not only provide us with long-term resources but will also enable us to leverage our ability to raise funds at competitive rates. It enhances our capacity to serve the needs of the lower-income micro, small and medium entrepreneurs.'

Crescent Standard Investment Bank Ltd has a diversified range of business activities in the areas of leasing, investment finance, housing finance, and asset management services.

Source: *Business Recorder*, 2005.

EXHIBIT 10

CASES IN CORPORATE GOVERNANCE 101

CSIBL-RELATED INVESTMENT COMPANIES

International House Financing Limited—Year Ended 30 June 2005 (Audited)

23 January 2006, press report: International Housing Finance Limited (IHFL) is a public limited company incorporated in Pakistan on 11 July 1990 under the Companies Ordinance, 1984. During the year under review, IHFL was formally listed on the Karachi Stock Exchange on 7 February 2005 and this Annual Report is the first after being listed.

The company is principally engaged in providing housing and non-residential finance facilities in Pakistan. The principal place of business is situated at 14-C, Main Gulberg, Jail Road, Lahore. Based on the financial results of the company for the year ended 30 June 2004, the JCR-VIS Credit Rating Company Limited upgraded the long-term credit rating of IHFL to 'BBB+' and the short-term rating to 'A-3.'

The company's paid up capital of Rs. 400 million as on 30 June 2005 was held by 811 shareholders, of which general public held 15 per cent. Shareholders holding more than 10 per cent include: Asian Stock Funds Limited (12.50 per cent), Crescent Leasing Corporation Limited (14.96 per cent) and Mr Manzurul Haq (10.09 per cent). Other Associated Companies namely Crescent Standard Investment Bank Limited, PICIC Commercial Bank Limited, and Safeway Mutual Funds Limited, together own nearly 9 per cent of the shares. The rest of the shares are held by corporate entities including banks and DFIs.

Number of IHFL employees as on 30 June 2005 was 56 (2004: 35).IFFL has seen small ups and downs but had been profitable in the past six years. It had also maintained growth in shareholders' equity. A summary of the key operating and financial data (2000–2005) published in the Annual Report for the year ended 30 June 2005, is given below.

[PAST PERFORMANCE]		(Rs. in 000)
FY-30 June	Profit/(Loss)	S. Equity
2000	10,400	131,214
2001	10,769	141,983
2002	8,911	150,894
2003	9,369	160,445
2004	15,602	270,008
2005	44,354	564,684

In terms of the notes to the financial statements, IHFL attempts to control credit risk by monitoring credit exposures, limiting transactions to specific counterparties, and continually assessing the credit worthiness of counterparties. IHFL seeks to manage its credit risk through diversification of financing activities to avoid undue concentrations of credit risk with individuals or groups of customers in specific locations or businesses. It also obtains securities considered appropriate. Composition of the housing/non-residential finance portfolio as on 30 June 2004 and 2005 is given below:

[Financing Portfolio]	% of Total	% of Total
Housing/Non-resi.–Gross	2005	2004
Financial Institutions	18%	24%
Health Care	6%	0%
Sugar	1%	3%
Mfg. and Trading	1%	2%
Educational Institutions	10%	4%
Others (incl. Individuals)	64%	67%
Total	100%	100%

In the notes pertaining to Contingencies, it has been stated that the Deputy Commissioner of Income Tax disallowed the penalty paid to the SBP amounting to Rs. 8.626 million as an inadmissible expense for the assessment year 2000–2001. The company filed an appeal first with the CIT (A) and later before the ITAT. Thereafter, the company has filed an appeal before the High Court of Sindh at Karachi against the decision of ITAT, which is currently pending for regular hearing.

EXHIBIT 10 (CONTINUED)

CASES IN CORPORATE GOVERNANCE 103

As a result of public offering of shares during the year under review the paid-up capital of the company step-up to Rs. 400 million compared to Rs. 200 million as at 30 June 2004. With the listing of the company the shareholders' equity stands at Rs. 565 million which will serve as a base for growth in the coming years.

According to Chief Executive's Review, IHFL approvals reached cumulatively Rs. 2.1 billion (Rs. 587 million for the year) and disbursement for the year touched a new high of Rs. 408 million up from Rs. 219 million of the previous year. The outstanding portfolio was Rs. 604 million, showing an increase of 90 per cent from Rs. 318 million at 30 June 2004. IHFL focus reportedly is to lend to the lower-income group—the sector which is most in need of finance if they are going to have a home of their own. At the end of June 2005, company's average residential loan outstanding was under Rs. 800,000.

During the year under review, IHFL acquired its own building for its head office in Lahore. These premises on Jail Road will also serve as the Northern Region's office and the company's training centre. The company opened its own offices in Islamabad and Hyderabad during the year and thus widened its operational reach.

The profit before tax for the year ended 30 June 2005 was Rs. 47.3 million as compared to Rs. 17.4 million for the year ended 30 June 2004. This profit also includes important contributions from the treasury as well as gain on disposal of an asset. The profit after tax at Rs. 44.3 million is the highest in the company's history and compares with profit after tax of Rs. 15.6 million for 2004. Comparative performance statistics for FY 2005 and FY 2004 are given below.

	(Audited)	**(Rs. in 000)**
Balance Sheet (On 30 June)	2005	2004
Total current assets:	398,952	131,911
Operating Fixed assets:	161,582	43,360
Housing finance facilities:	514,923	268,386
Total non current assets:	679,150	312,337
Total assets:	1,078,102	444,248
Total Current Liabilities:	357,634	82,521
Total capital employed:	720,468	361,727
Non current Liabilities:	91,352	84,933
Net assets:	629,116	276,794
Share capital:	400,000	200,000
Reserves:	164,684	70,008
Equity:	564,684	270,008
Surplus on revaluation-invest.:	1,055	3,087
Surplus on revaluation-FA:	63,377	3,699
Total equity:	629,116	276,794
Total Liabilities and Equity:	1,078,102	444,248
Ratios:		
Current Ratio:	1.12	1.6
Debt/Equity ratio:	0.60	1.01
Book Value per Share- Rs:	14.12	13.5
Market Value/share (06-01-06)- Rs:	8.6	-
Price/Book Value per share-X:	0.61	-
Bonus Shares Proposed:	12.50%	0.00%
Income Statement :		(Rs. in 000)
Year ended 30 June:	2005	2004
Income from housing finance:	63,131	43,529
Income from fund placement:	17,635	6,992
Income from investments:	6,506	2,100
Other income:	27,523	3,725
Total Income:	114,795	56,346

EXHIBIT 10 (CONTINUED)

CASES IN CORPORATE GOVERNANCE 105

Financial & Admn. Expenses:	66,318	37,492
Operating profit before provisions:	48,477	18,854
Provisions: Specific & general:	1,166	1,424
Profit before Taxation:	47,311	17,430
Taxation:	2,957	1,828
Profit after taxation:	44,354	15,602
Ratios:		
EPS (end of period capital)- Rs:	1.11	0.78

Operating profit/Total income:	42%	33%
Pre-tax profit/Total income:	41%	31%
After tax profit/Total income:	39%	28%
Return on Equity:	8%	6%
ROA:	4%	4%
ROCE:	6%	4%
Cash Flow Summary (Full Year)	2005	2004
Net Cash flow-Operating Activities:	207,034	-52,696
Net Cash Flow-Investing Activities:	-38,689	-49,434
Net Cash Flow-Financing Activities:	249,488	93,208
Change in net liquidity:	3,765	-8,922
Net liquidity at beginning:	20549	29471
Net liquidity at end:	24,314	20,549

COMPANY INFORMATION: Chairman: Altaf M. Saleem; Chief Executive: Manzurul Haq; Director: Roohi Raees Khan; Company Secretary: Usman Arshad; Chief Financial Officer: Muhammad Ali Siddiqui; Legal Advisors: Cornelius, Lane & Mufti, Advocates and Solicitors; Registered Office: 4th Floor, Crescent Standard Towers, 10-B, Block E-2, Gulberg III, Lahore; Head Office: 14-C, Main Gulberg, Jail Road, Lahore; Auditors: A.F. Ferguson & Company, Chartered Accountants; Web Address: www.ihfl.com.pk

Source: *Business Recorder*, 23 January 2006.

EXHIBIT 11

J. O. VOHRA CASE PREPARED BY SECP

Brief facts of this case are that on 1 February 2006, (Crescent Business Management Services (Pvt) Ltd) CSBM sold twenty (20) million shares of Crescent Standard Investment Bank Limited ('CSIBL') through First National Equities to Javed Omar Vohra & Co. Limited ('JOV') @ Rs. 12.00 per share [see Exhibit 8] and sold another four and a half (4.5) million shares to JOV on 3 February 2006 through Dossalani Securities @ Rs. 11.98 per share. Both CSIBL and JOV are listed public companies. Moreover, CSIBL and CSBM are associated companies as Mr Mahmood Ahmad is a director of both CSBM and CSIBL. He also held the position of chief executive in both the said companies at the time of aforementioned transactions.

On 3 October 2005, the Commission (SECP) commenced inspection of books and accounts of CSIBL; and in November, 2005, communicated to the Board of Directors of CSIBL critical information regarding mismanagement of books and accounts and unauthorized transactions undertaken by CSIBL, as well as the poor financial condition of CSIBL, asking it to explain and clarify the same.

On 28 November 2005, the CSIBL Board of Directors held a meeting to discuss the findings of the Commission's inspection and the queries put forward to them for reply and clarification; and as of that date (if not earlier), all directors of CSIBL attending the said meeting (including Mr Mahmood Ahmad as both director and chief executive) clearly came into possession of material non-public information regarding the frail and deteriorating financial condition of CSIBL.After the CSIBL's Board decision taken in its meeting of 28 November 2005 to merge the hitherto parallel books of accounts; which had been unlawfully maintained separately in CSIBL, the consequent consolidation of CSIBL's accounts showed that losses had wiped out most of its equity capital.

Information regarding the abovementioned affairs of CSIBL was not generally available and while being in possession of such material non-public information regarding CSIBL, CSBM dealt in the securities of CSIBL and started selling its shareholding in CSIBL in early February 2006, importantly making the aforementioned transactions of sale of CSIBL shares to JOV totaling twenty four and a half (24.5) million shares as stated in the first paragraph above.

EXHIBIT 11 (CONTINUED)

CASES IN CORPORATE GOVERNANCE 107

After the sale of shares to JOV, the price of CSIBL shares materially dropped as the above mentioned information regarding CSIBL's affairs became public and, as of the date of this order, it had already touched as low as Rs. 4.55 per share.

It was thus apparent that on the basis of unpublished price-sensitive information, CSBM dealt in CSIBL securities and managed to cause JOV to purchase CSIBL securities from CSBM thereby itself avoiding loss and causing the same to JOV—which acts of CSBM fell within the ambit of insider trading defined and proscribed by Chapter III-A of the Securities and Exchange Ordinance, 1969 ('the Ordinance').

In light of the foregoing, on 5 April 2006, Show Cause Notices ('SCN') were issued to the Board of Directors of CSBM comprising only two directors—namely Mr Mahmood Ahmad and Siyyid Tahir Nawazish—which summed up the allegations against CSBM in the following manner:

a) CSBM sold securities of CSIBL while being associated with CSIBL through a common director and in possession of material non-public information related to CSIBL.

b) CSBM sold to JOV 24.5 million shares at Rupees 12.00 and 11.98 per share on 1 and 3 February 2006, respectively and the share price of CSIBL declined to Rupees 8.00 per share on 13 March 2006; and

c) CSBM, by acting on material non-public information, illegally caused JOV to deal in securities of CSIBL in violation of section 15A of the Ordinance,[7] and thus avoided a loss and inflicted loss on JOV and its shareholders.

Source: SECP.

---

7   Securities and Exchange Ordinance, 1969: INSIDER TRADING 15-A. Prohibition on stock exchange deals by insiders. No person who is, or has been, at any time during the preceding six months, associated with a company shall, directly or indirectly, deal on a stock exchange in any listed securities of that or any other company or cause any other person to deal in securities of such company, if he has information which:
a   is not generally available;
b) would, if it were so available, be likely to materially affect the price of those securities; or
c) relates to any transaction (actual or contemplated) involving such company.
    Explanation—For the purpose of this section, the expression "associated with" shall mean a person associated with a company, if he-(i) is an officer or employee of that company or an associated company; or (ii) occupies a position which gives him access thereto by reason of any professional or business relationship between him or his employer or a company or associated company of which he is a director.

This section contains cases dealing with various management situations and how these were handled with by the companies concerned.

CASES IN MANAGEMENT PRACTICES

2.1 ENGRO CHEMICALS PAKISTAN LIMITED— BUSINESS DISASTER OVERCOME

CASE HIGHLIGHTS AND KEY POINTS

Engro Chemicals Pakistan Limited (Engro) was a very large manufacturer and marketer of fertilizer in Pakistan. It had a number of subsidiaries and joint ventures in a variety of businesses. The company was listed on the Karachi Stock Exchange (KSE) and was among the top companies as ranked by the KSE. In August 2007, the company's head office that was located in one of the prestigious buildings of Karachi, called the PNSC building, was completely destroyed by a fire. The office fire destroyed all the equipment as well as the hardcopies of the accounting records. The company was suddenly faced with a catastrophic loss as the records were critical to Engro's day to day operations. What followed was the painful process of business continuity and disaster recovery as Engro team bravely fought round the clock to bring their mission-critical processes back on track.

The information technology (IT) department had developed a disaster recovery plan (DRP) in 2005 that was exclusively related to re-establishing the IT facilities after any event that could make the business systems inoperable. The company invoked the DRP as soon as the news of the complete destruction of the office facilities was received. The IT and finance staff had to use the backup equipment and data files to restart the transaction processing. The case includes a description of various business systems used by Engro and the data security processes that had enabled the company to restore the accounting and other systems needed at its head office. The main teaching objective was to focus on minimizing the business risks arising due to the destruction of the IT facilities. The case also has details of the DRP, which can be analysed as to its contents, and examination of the details of the management processes of Engro allows for a discussion on corporate governance within the company.

POTENTIAL USES OF THE CASE

This case can be used in an MBA or executive program in which the teaching objective is to highlight the need for a disaster recovery plan (DRP) as part of an organization's business risk minimization strategy. With the increasing importance of information technology (IT) for the continuation of critical business functions, combined with a transition to a 24-hour economy, the importance of protecting an organization's data and IT infrastructure in the event of a disruptive situation has become an increasing concern in recent years.

The case can also be used in a class on IT in which the teaching objective is to discuss the issues related to IT security. This includes identifying threats that face an organization:

- Malicious attacks by employees or by third parties via the Internet.

- Total destruction due to a natural or unexpected disaster.

IT security gaps include the vulnerabilities in computing hardware or software. They indirectly invite malicious hackers to work on and exploit them. Security holes are flaws in the network software that allow unintended control within the network. Network components such as personal computers (PCs) and routers can contain these vulnerable areas in their operating systems. Therefore, the technical details of any system should not be made public unless absolutely necessary.

DISASTER RECOVERY PLANNING

Disaster recovery planning consists of the process, policies and procedures related to a recovery or continuation of technological infrastructure critical to an organization after a natural or man-made disaster causing destruction.

1. Natural disasters: Preventing a natural disaster is impossible, but it is possible to take precautions to avoid losses. These disasters include floods, fires, earthquakes, hurricanes, and other such phenomena.

2. Man-made disasters: These disasters are major causes for disruption in a company's normal operations. Human error and intervention may be intentional or unintentional and can cause massive failures such as loss of office facilities, communication, and utility. These disasters include accidents, fires, walkouts, sabotage, burglary, viruses, intrusions, etc.

Disaster recovery planning is a subset of a larger process known as business continuity planning and should include planning for resumption of applications, data, hardware, communications (such as networking), and other IT infrastructure. A business continuity plan (BCP) includes planning for non-IT related aspects such as key personnel, facilities, crisis communication, and reputation protection: it should refer to the DRP for IT-related infrastructure recovery and continuity.

The company had a DRP for its IT section that had been designed for use in the event that the IT systems became inoperative due to a disaster. It was helpful in ensuring that the recovery and reestablishment of mission-critical accounting control systems was possible in an organized manner and in as little time as possible.

ASSIGNMENT QUESTIONS

1. What were the risks faced by Engro after the fire had left its head office in ruins?

2. Explain the purpose of the DRP. What features were omitted from the plan?

3. The systems were not integrated and this made it simpler for Engro to recover from the disaster: does this negate the concept of enterprise resource planning (ERP)? Why, in your opinion did Engro deviate from the DRP?

4. Evaluate the overall plan and implementation.

CASE TEXT: ENGRO CHEMICALS PAKISTAN LIMITED— BUSINESS DISASTER OVERCOME

On 20 October 2007, Ruhail Mohammed, vice-president and chief financial officer (CFO) of Engro Chemical Pakistan Limited (Engro) was preparing his notes to present at the management committee meeting on 1 November 2007. A critical item on the agenda was that on 19 August 2007, a fire in the PNSC building which housed the Engro head office, had destroyed a substantial portion of the company's hard-copy records relating to the financial years 2004/05 and 2005/06, as well as the period from 1 January 2007, to August 2007; however, the electronic data had remained largely intact. The end of the company's financial year was 31 December and the external auditors were due to commence their work in December 2007, as the deadline to publish the annual financial report was 20 February 2008. The company was listed on the Karachi Stock Exchange (KSE) and, being a blue chip company, had informed the stock exchange of the date it would announce its final results for 2007.

Mohammed had to update the management committee on the progress that had been made under a plan according to which the company's critical accounting and control systems and data would be restored, so as to keep company operations uninterrupted. The auditors had pointed out that since they had earlier conducted a review of the financial records as of 30 June 2007, they would rely on that work and not need any records for the first six months. Their main focus would be on the second half of the year, and this would require that the company provide them with all the information that they requested in order to form an opinion for the annual audit report. As the records for 2005/06 were also destroyed, they were concerned that the company could be in breach of the statutory provisions in the Companies Ordinance[1] relating to the minimum period that a publicly-listed company's records were required to be retained. Engro was launching a number of new projects and the auditors needed to be satisfied that the plans would not be affected by the loss of records. The CFO was confident in the company's documented disaster recovery plan (DRP) that had been activated and he felt that matters were under control.

COMPANY BACKGROUND

Engro Chemical Pakistan Ltd. had been incorporated in 1965 as Esso Pakistan Fertilizer Company Ltd. The core business of Engro was the manufacturing and marketing of fertilizers and it was the second largest producer of urea in the country, which was produced at the plant site in Daharki (a small town 570 kilometers from Karachi). Engro also produced NPK[2] (*Zarkhez*) at the plant in Port Qasim, a few kilometers from Karachi, and marketed two other brands of fertilizer: (MAP) under the brand name *Zorawar*, and DAP. Owing to the continuously declining margins in seed business, the management had decided to exit from this business in a phased manner. This demonstrated the management's proactive business approach of conducting a continuous review of operations and realigning corporate strategy according to changing business dynamics.

During 2007, all of Engro's businesses grew rapidly. The principal business of the company remained in the manufacturing and marketing of fertilizers. Its joint ventures and subsidiary companies were engaged in a variety of businesses: chemical terminals and storage, PVC resin manufacturing and marketing, control and automation, foods and energy businesses. A brief review of the main business and the new projects underway follows:

1　The corporate sector in Pakistan is governed by the Companies Ordinance 1984, which was promulgated on 8 October 1984 and major amendments made via the Companies (Amendment) Ordinance, 2002. The objectives of the Companies Ordinance 1984 were inter alia to consolidate and amend the law relating to companies and certain other associations for the purpose of healthy growth of corporate enterprises, protection of investors and creditors, promotion of investment and development of economy. The detailed provisions of the Companies Ordinance, 1984 sought to meet these objectives and have been amended and updated from time to time to keep in line with the changing circumstances.

2　NPK is a fertilizer consisting of nitrogen, phosphorus and potassium.

The fertilizer sold by the company was of two types:

Urea: During 2007, a total of 4.76 million tons of urea was produced in the country, of which Engro produced 954,000 tons while in the process of further expansion. The urea plant expansion was the largest private sector investment that had been made in the history of Pakistan. In 2007, it was on track for completion in 2010, and with key contracts and financing in place, the construction work had begun.

Phosphates: Engro sales up to the third-quarter of 2007 indicated that it would be in a good position as the market leader, as it expected to capture 35 per cent of the phosphates market for the full year. This fertilizer was imported and its price was susceptible to fluctuations in the international market.

The activities of subsidiary and joint venture companies were as follows:

Engro Polymer & Chemicals Ltd (EPCL): This subsidiary was involved in the manufacturing and sales of poly vinyl chloride (PVC) and was also being expanded. Its backward integration project was expected to be completed by mid-2009.

Engro Vopak Terminal Ltd (EVTL): This was a 50:50 joint venture with Royal Vopak of the Netherlands. This subsidiary had commenced building the country's first cryogenic ethylene storage facility.

Avanceon: Engro owned 63 per cent of Avanceon, which was a leader in industrial automation business. It had acquired facilities in the United States and was in the process of seeking to serve customers as an offshore outsourced vendor.

Engro Foods Limited (EFL): This was a wholly-owned subsidiary of Engro and 2007 was its first complete year of operations. It had continued its expansion by adding to its brand portfolio, milk production and distribution capacity.

Engro Energy (Pvt) Ltd: This was also a wholly-owned subsidiary of Engro and had concluded the formalities to set up an innovative and cost-effective power plant: their target was to add 217 megawatts to the national grid.

Engro Eximp (Pvt) Ltd: This was a wholly-owned subsidiary of Engro and was engaged in the trading of phosphatic fertilizers.

Engro was publicly listed on the three stock exchanges in Pakistan: Karachi, Lahore and Islamabad. Its earnings had grown steadily over the last 10 years (see Exhibit 1), as shown by the increasing trend in the annual earnings per share (see Exhibit 2).

A leading Pakistani business conglomerate known as the Dawood Group (DG) held the majority 42 per cent of shares in Engro, while the ownership of Engro employees and employee trust shareholding was eight per cent. Engro's board of directors comprised five members from its own management: two from DG and three other non-executive directors (see Exhibit 3). During 2006, Hussain Dawood—chairman of DG—was elected as the chairman of Engro. The association of DG which also owned other chemical businesses, had augmented the capacity of the board to guide the management in formulating its long-term strategy.

MANAGEMENT

The company was managed through the following principle management committees:

Board Compensation Committee: This committee was responsible for reviewing and recommending all the elements of compensation, organization and employee development policies relating to the executives and approving all matters relating to remuneration of executive directors and members of the management committee. This committee (see Exhibit 3) consisted mainly of non-executive directors and had met four times during 2007.

Board Audit Committee: This committee consisted of four independent non-executive directors (see Exhibit 3). The chief executive officer (CEO) and the CFO only attended if they were invited. As part of its work, the committee met with the external auditors at least once per year. During 2007, this committee had met seven times and had been informed by the CFO of the data loss the company had incurred and that the DRP was being implemented.

In addition, the following committees were set up at the operational level and functioned in advisory capacity in order to provide recommendations to the CEO relating to business and employee matters.

Corporate HSE Committee: This committee was responsible for providing leadership and strategic guidance on all health, safety and environment (HSE) improvement initiatives and was responsible for monitoring compliance against regulatory standards and selected international benchmarks.

Management Committee: This committee was responsible for reviewing and endorsing long-term strategic plans, capital and expenses budgets, development and stewardship of business plans and reviewing the effectiveness of the risk management processes and the system of internal control (see Exhibit 3).

COED Committee: This committee was responsible for the review of compensation, organization and employee development (COED) matters for all employees excluding directors and executives.

BUSINESS RISKS

During 2007, the management committee undertook a review of the major financial and operating risks faced by the company. Internal controls were recognized by the company as being an important responsibility of the board of directors. As no system could be totally risk-free, the company recognized that the system of controls was there to minimize risk of material misstatement or loss, but could not eliminate it completely. The detailed design and operation of the system of internal control had been delegated to the CEO while the board retained the overall responsibility of the risks involved. The control framework consisted of:

- Clear organization structure.

- Established authority limits and accountabilities.

- Well-understood policies and procedures.

- Budgeting and review processes.

The external and internal auditors' reports were received by the board audit committee (BAC), and the managing committee reviewed the processes and ensured that the controls were effective.

BUSINESS CONTROL SYSTEMS

Engro's business transaction data processing and communications was based on using information technology (IT) resources at two locations:

1. Head office in PNSC Building at Karachi.

2. Plant site at Daharki, which was 570 kilometers away.

All systems were linked so that the IT applications installed on servers in the head office were being accessed by users at various locations:

- Daharki plant;

- Zarkhez plant at Port Qasim;

- Other regional offices.

IT INFRASTRUCTURE AT HEAD OFFICE

The IT assets at the head office consisted of computer equipment linked via an online data communication network on which different application systems were being used. The company staff occupied three floors, in the multistory PNSC building, and computer users were spread over all three floors. Computing equipment on each of these floors was connected by means of a fibre optics backbone and each floor had its own network control equipment such as switches. The head office was also connected to different locations through a wide area network (WAN) (see Exhibit 4). The details of these links for various locations were as follows:

- 256 kilobits per second (kbps) DXX[3] link with plant site at Daharki.

- 64 kbps radio link with Zarkhez plant at Port Qasim.

- 64 kbps DXX link with regional office at Multan.

- 64 kbps DXX link with regional office at Hyderabad.

- 64 kbps data link with regional office at Lahore.

The server room was on the seventh floor where all communication links terminated on to the central router in that room.

Engro's two joint venture companies EPCL and EVTL had their head offices close to Engro in the Bahria Complex[4]. Systems of these two companies were also connected with the Engro network by a digital subscriber line (DSL) link through a firewall mainly for exchanging e-mails with Engro and to access the Internet.

There were two Internet connections: one with the Internet service provider (ISP) CyberNet over radio link for Internet bound e-mails and connectivity with Lahore regional office, the other based on DSL technology with the ISP Multinet and being used for Internet traffic. A firewall was used to protect Engro's network from various Internet threats.

The following Engro communication and financial application systems were located at the head office:

- Lotus Notes-based e-mail system.

---

3   *Digital cross-connect*: A network device used by telecom carriers and large enterprises to switch and multiplex low-speed voice and data signals onto high-speed lines and vice versa. It is typically used to aggregate several T1 lines into a higher-speed electrical or optical line as well as to distribute signals to various destinations; for example, voice and data traffic may arrive at the cross-connect on the same facility, but be destined for different carriers. Voice traffic would be transmitted out one port, while data traffic goes out another. Cross-connects come large and small, handling only a few ports up to a few thousand. Narrowband, wideband and broadband cross-connects support channels down to DS0, DS1 and DS3 respectively.

4   Bahria Complex was a set of office buildings, owned by the Pakistan Navy, in which various companies had rented space for their offices.

- MIDAS system for sales.

- SAP ERP system (see Exhibit 5) for accounting transactions.

IT INFRASTRUCTURE AT DAHARKI PLANT

All the key buildings at the Daharki plant were connected through optical fibre backbone and each building had its own network equipment. All servers were located in a server room which was located in the administration building. The Daharki network was connected to the head office network by a data communication link. This link was based on DXX technology and consisted of a last mile radio link between the plant and the local Daharki telephone exchange. The staff at the Daharki plant connected to the router in the server room over dial-up telephone lines to access the Internet.

APPLICATION SYSTEMS AT HEAD OFFICE

E-mail Setup

Engro's e-mail system was based on IBM's Lotus Domino technology, and Lotus Notes was used as a front-end client to access the e-mail server (see Exhibit 4). Users in the Karachi office, Zarkhez plant, and all the regional offices except the Daharki region accessed the e-mail server in the head office.

The head office server was connected to the e-mail server in Daharki over a wide area network (WAN). It was also connected to EVTL and EPCL's e-mail servers over a DSL-based virtual private network (VPN) link. All Internet e-mails for Engro Karachi staff, plant staff at Daharki, and regional office users EVTL, EPCL, and EFL were received by the head office server through a firewall. Similarly, all outgoing e-mails were sent to the relay server by the e-mail server at the head office. The Engro infrastructure was used by a number of subsidiaries to route their business communications.

MIDAS Setup

MIDAS was an in-house application developed using Oracle Developer, linking to the back-end Oracle database. MIDAS used two servers in the head office: an application server and a database server. The head office users accessed the database server through the Oracle client directly while all remote users (regional offices and Zarkhez plant staff) accessed MIDAS through the application server via an Internet browser. There was one MIDAS server at the plant, which was accessed by the plant distribution department for the detailing of urea orders to the truckers and for processing their invoices.

Key activities performed by different users through MIDAS at the head office were the following:

- Master data (new-product setup, urea pricing).

- Bank guarantee handling.

- Management of dealers account.

- Payroll allowance entry.

- Product shipment from the port and Zarkhez plant.

- Monthly closing.

All information entered in the head-office MIDAS server was automatically replicated to the plant MIDAS server using a replication feature created by Oracle. Similarly, any information entered at the plant (such as trucker detailing, etc.) was replicated to the head-office MIDAS database server automatically.

SAP Setup

SAP was being used by the finance and human resource (HR) sections at the head office and by the Industrial Relations Department at the plant to facilitate their operational needs (see

Exhibit 5). Only two modules of SAP—namely HR and financial control (FICO)—were in use on the Red Hat Linux Advanced Server operating system. The following key tasks were performed using SAP at head office:

- Accounts payable (invoice processing, payments, vendor payment, cash receipts, cheque printing).

- General ledger.

- Financial control.

- Asset management.

- Payroll processing (all Engro employees).

- Compensation and benefit administration (all Engro employees).

APPLICATION SYSTEMS AT PLANT

The applications installed on servers at the Daharki plant were accessed mainly by users at the plant, consisting of the following systems:

- MAXIMO computerized maintenance management system (CMMS), also used by the purchasing section at the head office.

- MIDAS sales and distribution system, which was used to update the shipments of goods and other related information.

- E-mail systems.

MAXIMO SETUP

MAXIMO was a state of the art CMMS software system used by various organizations worldwide for computer-based maintenance management: this system was installed at the Engro plant. The main modules that were used kept a detailed record of company assets, controlled the use of the stores and spares inventories, and assisted in purchasing functions. The manufacturing division located at the plant and the purchasing section located at the head office used this software extensively. All other departments that used MAXIMO were at the plant: maintenance, operations and technology, and the warehouse section.

DISASTER RECOVERY PLAN

As the August 2007 fire at Engro head office had spread very quickly, it destroyed everything, including all desktop computers and high-performance servers that contained daily business transaction data. Earlier in 2005, as part of a risk mitigation effort, the IT department had developed a DRP to recover from a disaster (see Exhibit 6). In accordance with the DRP instructions, the plan was activated by Mohammed on 20 August, as the company senior management realized that quick actions were required by all concerned.

TEMPORARY OFFICES

The IT department consisted of two sections, each with its own particular skill: one section was dedicated to managing the IT infrastructure, and the other consisted of functional specialists dealing with information systems (IS) applications (SAP, MAXIMO, and MIDAS). The DRP required that the recovery site be at the Daharki plant where spare servers similarly configured to the destroyed servers had been kept for use in an emergency. Management revised the plan, however, by deciding to use the following four locations:

1. Engro guest houses in Karachi: There were two guest houses, one of which became a base for HR functions and the executives, while the other became a temporary base for accounting and other transactional functions.

2. Engro plant at Daharki: The sales accounting staff that used the internally-developed MIDAS system were moved there as the complete backup of MIDAS and the necessary computing capacity was already in place.

3. Engro Polymer offices at the Bahria building in Karachi: The backup servers kept at Daharki, with SAP software already installed, were brought to the Bahria building in order to set up the critical accounting systems. The related staff were also shifted to the offices of this subsidiary company. As there was a computing infrastructure already available, Engro's e-mail system was expected to become functional quickly, establishing all communication as before.

The IT infrastructure staff then had to make sure that adequate computing facilities were available. This was a monumental task, as sophisticated servers and other peripherals were required quickly. They asked their key vendor, Inbox Business Technologies (Pvt) Limited (Inbox) for assistance and Inbox staff worked closely with Engro IT staff to re-establish the infrastructure. The Inbox team ensured timely and swift delivery of the required services, workstations, laptops, low-end servers, wireless LAN/WAN, uninterruptible power supplies (UPS), printers, and other necessary products.

DATA RECOVERY

The Engro core accounting system consisted of the following:

1. Three modules of SAP (HR, financial accounting (FI) and controlling (CO), the last two jointly referred to as FICO).

2. The MIDAS system.

3. The MAXIMO system.

The top priority was to make all the SAP modules operational on the backup servers at the Engro Polymer offices in Karachi. The sales system, MIDAS, was being operated from the plant in Daharki where all the head office sales staff had relocated. MAXIMO was located at the plant and had not been affected by the disaster.

The backup regime for SAP applications data had consisted of saving copies of the data on a weekly, monthly, and annual basis using tapes that were stored at an off-site location. The data was also backed up on tapes by the IT staff on a daily basis and kept in the head office in a fire-proof storage cabinet. On a weekly basis, the tape relating to the last business day in the week was sent off-site for storage.

The daily backup was destroyed as it was in the head office building. Some data relating to a short period of time was also lost due to corruption of weekly data tapes and this had to be carefully identified and recreated.

The MIDAS sales system was installed at the head office and at Daharki. The backup regime, in addition to daily, weekly, and monthly tape backups, included the data synchronization between head office and Daharki servers using Oracle's replication feature, so that there was complete backup available at both locations. Hence the sales staff were sent to Daharki to use the MIDAS system from there.

Accounting records that were destroyed included the physical records such as vendor invoices, contracts, and working papers.

Engro used an outsourced service provider for processing the share and corporate secretarial records, therefore protecting that information. After setting up temporary offices, the company then launched an initiative to recreate significant lost records for the period 1 January 2007, onwards.

EXTERNAL AUDIT

The external auditors were due to carry out their final audit checks in December, and the senior accounts advisor Farhan Akram, who was in charge of recreating the documents related to SAP, was confident that the documents supporting the transactions data for the period of January to 19 August 2007 would be fully recreated. He had split his finance team located at the guest house into two sections:

1. Day-to-day accounting staff: The ongoing daily business transactions related to accounting of sales and purchases were processed on the reinstalled systems, including MIDAS, MAXIMO, and SAP. This was facilitated by the re-established electronic links, e-mail, and Internet in the Bahria building office. As the systems were not fully integrated, their restart and recovery was simpler than if all the systems had been integrated.

2. Data recreation staff: One of the leading public accounting firms was hired to provide temporary accounting staff who had four to five years of training experience. This staff was given the specific task of reconciling duplicate invoices received from all major vendors. Once the veracity had been thoroughly checked, the documents were passed on to Engro employees for entry into the SAP modules. Similarly, the payment records for the lost data were obtained from the banks that were used for payment, and after checking and reconciling this data, the payments were entered in the systems. Data had to be recreated only for SAP applications and that too was facilitated as the company was able to obtain the records from its banks.

The company found the process of generating document records to be a tedious and time-consuming task requiring external resources, and it was therefore decided that only the current year's data needed to be recreated, as it was necessary for the year's audit. The company felt that there would be no purpose in incurring a huge cost for regenerating physical documents, as the prior years' records had been audited and the data was safe in electronic form. The company had also informed their taxation office, the Large Taxpayers Unit, of the fire and its consequences.

The auditors insisted that the physical records for 2005 and 2006 would be required, as Companies Ordinance stipulated that data must be kept for 10 years. They said that a qualified audit opinion stating noncompliance with the statutory regulations related to historic data would be given.

CORPORATE GOVERNANCE AT ENGRO

In its draft annual report for 2007, the company intended to include the compliance statement required for statutory purposes. This specifically addressed the following areas:

Risk Management Process

In 2007, a major review of the financial and operating risks facing the company was undertaken by the management committee. As soon as the fire broke out and it was clear that the office accounting records would be destroyed, the company activated its DRP which was developed by the IT section in 2005.

Internal Control Framework

The board audit committee received the reports on the system of internal controls from the external and internal auditors and also reviewed the process of monitoring the internal controls. The internal audit function carried out reviews on the financial, operational and compliance controls and reported the findings to the CEO and divisional management. The annual internal audit program was based on an annual risk assessment of the operating areas. The board audit committee approved the audit program and during the year, it received reports related to all material issues which were discovered.

There was a company-wide policy regarding approval of investment expenditure and asset disposals and post-completion reviews were performed on all material investment expenditure.

CONCLUSION

Mohammed assessed the situation and started writing his report for the meeting. It began, 'All computers and the data on them in the head office was destroyed and the company has had to rely on backup copies of the data.' Mohammed related the following data recreation steps:

- A core team had been formed which analyzed gaps in the electronic data.

- Help had been obtained from a public accounting firm, which provided temporary accounting staff.

- Banks, through which payments had been made, were approached to obtain copies of their records.

- All key vendors had been asked to send duplicate invoices.

- Data consisting of the necessary details was being re-entered into the related SAP modules based on the cut-off date.

The meeting of the management committee on 1 November was the regularly scheduled meeting, but Mohammed knew that all senior management was concerned over the tremendous loss of entire office facilities and that they were scrutinizing the progress of data recovery. He felt that simply focusing on the accounting data was inadequate, as the destruction had been catastrophic and the entire office had been destroyed. The board audit committee had suggested that Mohammed start working to create comprehensive security policies to manage all kinds of business risk. The DRP was related to the IT section only and it was clear that the plan would need to be revised to cover other areas of business operations. Mohammed wanted to address the various aspects of how the DRP was to be converted into a business continuity plan. He was writing a brief report on the steps that had been taken and those that were planned. A new office building had been chosen and alterations to meet Engro's requirements were to begin: Mohammed wanted to list the key risk factors that had to be met by the new office building.

EXHIBIT 1

ENGRO CHEMICAL PAKISTAN LIMITED: RECENT PERFORMANCE

(in millions of rupees)

	Half Year 2007	2006	2005	2004	2003	2002	2001	2000
Net sales revenue	9,031	17,602	18,276	12,798	11,884	10,620	8,006	8,080
Operating profit	1,230	2,756	2,641	2,233	2,534	2,327	1,736	1,914
Profit before tax	997	3,445	3,220	2,315	2,323	1,836	1,191	1,350
Profit after tax	650	2,547	2,319	1,611	1,557	1,133	1,064	1,126
Employee costs		950	804	795	749	673	594	544
Taxes, duties and development surcharge		4,633	4,168	3,911	3,457	3,062	2,266	1,762
Workers funds		251	215	156	168	113	69	71
Assets and Liabilities								
Property, plant and equipment	10,770	6,318	6,351	6,492	6,648	6,865	6,643	6,462
Capital expenditure		391	377	520	370	823	435	578
Long-term investments	5,056	1,480	748	-	85	-	-	--
Long-term liabilities	8,840	1,800	2,890	2,580	3,236	3,323	2,992	3,070
Net current assets	1,871	2,042	2,211	1,618	1,796	1,252	1,194	993
Dividends And Shares								
Shareholders' funds	8,248	9,370	7,376	6,586	6,199	5,817	5,727	5,582
Shares at year-end (millions)	na	168	153	153	153	139	139	121
Dividend per share (rupees)	na	9.0	11.0	8.5	8.0	7.5	7.5	7.0
Dividend payout ratio	na	59%	73%	81%	79%	92%	98%	75%
Bonus shares	na	0	0	0	0	10%	0%	15%
Engro urea production (thousands of metric tons)	na	969	912	870	955	852	790	808

EXHIBIT 1 (CONTINUED)

Engro urea sales (thousands of metric tons)	na	945	890	891	930	846	779	800
Zarkez/Engro NP (thousands of metric tons)	na	108	157	121	72	73	31	0

Source: Company financial statements.

EXHIBIT 2

CASES IN MANAGEMENT PRACTICES 131

ANNUAL EARNINGS PER SHARE

Amount in rupees	2004 (restated)	2005 (restated)	2006 (restated)	2007 (restated)
Earnings per share	10.12	13.82	15.13	16.51
Dividend per share	8.50	11.00	9.00	7.00

Source: Company records.

PRINCIPAL BOARD COMMITTEES AND MEMBERS

Name	Title	Board Compensation Committee	Board Audit Committee
Hussain Dawood	Chairman Non-executive director	Member	
Shabbir Hashmi	Non-executive director	Member	Member
Arshad Nasar	Non-executive director	Member	Member
Asad Umar	Chief executive officer	Member	
Shahzada Dawood	Non-executive director		Member
Isar Ahmad	Non-executive director		Member

Source: Company records.

PRINCIPAL OPERATION COMMITTEES AND MEMBERS

Name	Title in Engro	Management Committee	Corporate HSE Committee	COED Committee
Asad Umar	Chief executive officer	Member (chairman)	Member	Member
Asif Qadir	Senior vice-president	Member	Member	Member
Khalid S.Subhani	Senior vice-president-manufacturing	Member	Member	Member
Khalid Mansoor	Senior vice-president	Member	Member	Member
Khalid Mir	General manager-marketing	Member	Member	Member
Andalib Alavi	General manager Legal and company secretary	Member		
S.Imran ul Haq	Vice-president	Member	Member	Member
Syed Ahsan Uddin	Vice-president		Member	
Sarfaraz A.Rehman	Chief executive officer–Engro Foods Limited		Member	
Ruhail Mohammed	Chief financial officer	Member	Member	Member
Asif Tajik	General manager–manufacturing- Daharki	Member	Member	Member
Imranullah Naveed Khan	General manager of expansion project	Member	Member	Member
Tahir Jawaid	General manager-Human resources and public affairs	Member	Member	

Source: Company records.

SYSTEMS INFRASTRUCTURE

Network at Head Office

ECPL Network Infrastructure

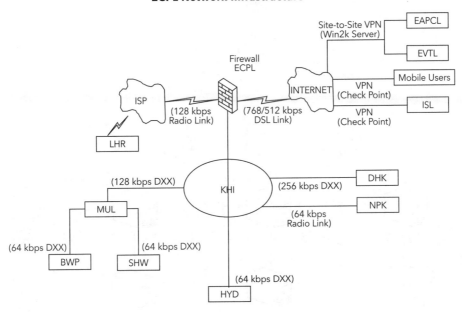

Figure 2.2

MIDAS

Figure 2.2

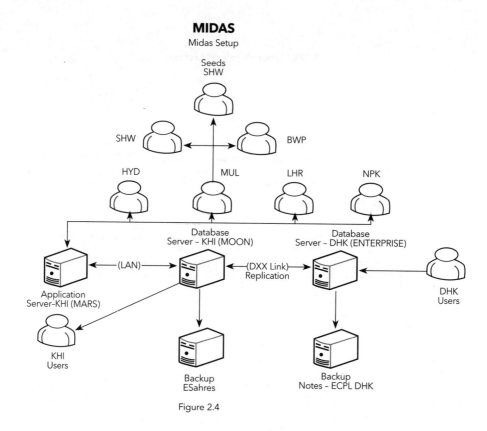

Figure 2.4

EXHIBIT 4 (CONTINUED)

EMAIL AT HEAD OFFICE

Email Setup

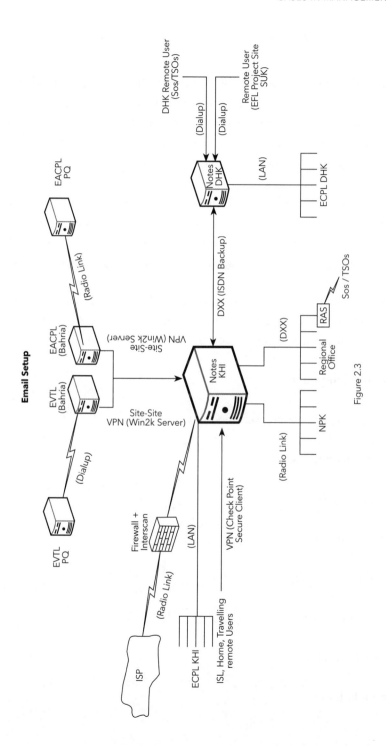

Figure 2.3

Source: Company records.

SAP MODULES: FI AND CO

The SAP FI module has the capability of meeting all the accounting and financial needs of an organization. It is within this module that financial managers as well as other managers within your business can review the financial position of the company in real-time, as opposed to legacy systems, which often requires overnight updates before financial statements can be generated and run for management review.

The real-time functionality of the SAP modules allow for better decision-making and strategic planning. The FI module integrates with other SAP modules such as materials management, production planning, sales and distribution, plant maintenance and project systems.

The FI Module also integrates with HR, which includes personnel management, time management, and travel management. Payroll transactions occurring within the specific modules generate account postings via account determination tables.

The FI Module Components

The FI Module comprises several sub-modules as follows:

- Accounts receivables.

- Accounts payable.

- Asset accounting.

- Special purpose ledger.

- Travel management.

- Bank accounting.

- Consolidation.

EXHIBIT 5 (CONTINUED)

CASES IN MANAGEMENT PRACTICES 137

- Funds management.

- General ledger.

The SAP CO module provides supporting information to management for the purpose of planning, reporting, and monitoring the operations of their business. Management decision-making can be achieved with the level of information provided by this module.

Components of the CO module are as follows:

- Cost element accounting.

- Cost centre accounting.

- Internal orders.

- Activity-based costing (ABC).

- Product cost controlling.

- Profitability analysis.

- Profit centre accounting.

Note: The above exhibit lists all the functionality of SAP, not all of which was being used by Engro.
Source: SAP literature.

EXTRACT FROM THE IT DISASTER RECOVERY PLAN

1.2   Objective:

The primary objective of this Disaster Recovery Plan (DRP) is to document the various recovery steps to be followed in order to resume key IT operations as quickly as possible, in the following scenarios:

1.   Disaster at head office (making the location unavailable for use)

2.   Disaster at Daharki server room/administration building (making the Daharki (DHK) IT setup unavailable for use)

1.3   Scope:

The DRP acts as a working document in the event of the above-mentioned disaster scenarios and provides specific routines for action that will assist in the early and effective response to disaster(s).

This document does not provide any plans for:

- The recovery of business functions/operations other than IT

  Circumstances that produce the following results shall indicate a disaster situation for Engro:

  - Non-availability of MIDAS at Karachi or Daharki for one week

  - Non-availability of MAXIMO at Karachi of Daharki for one week

  - Non-availability of SAP for one week

EXHIBIT 6 (CONTINUED)

CASES IN MANAGEMENT PRACTICES 139

Engro IT DRP (extracts)

Assumption: Head office building is not available for use as a result of a disaster (such as a fire incident, an earthquake, or an act of terrorism).

Key points of the plan:

1. DHK plant site shall be used as recovery site for IT applications.

2. Only MIDAS, MAXIMO, and SAP applications shall be made available to the organization for usage at the recovery site.

3. Key users of SAP, MIDAS, and MAXIMO shall move to the DHK recovery site.

4. An IT recovery team will be formed that will supervise all DRP related activities.

5. SAP recovery team shall be responsible for the recovery of SAP.

6. MIDAS recovery team shall be responsible for the recovery of MIDAS.

7. The following measures have been taken to minimize the recovery time:

    a. Spare servers have been placed at the DHK plant site in the security building outside plant (to be used to recover SAP, MIDAS, and MAXIMO).

    b. Complete backup of SAP (FICO and HR modules) and MIDAS system is sent to recovery site on tape cartridges on a weekly basis.

Limitations:

1. No e-mails within as well as outside the organization for head office, Zarkhez plant, and all regional office users (excluding DHK).

2. No Internet e-mail exchange for DHK, EFL project site, SUK (Engro Foods plant at Sukkur), EVTL, EPCL, and regional office DHK users.

Invoking the Plan:

Following Individuals are authorized to invoke the IT services recovery plan in case of disaster at head office:

1. Chief Executive Officer   –   Engro

2. GM Finance & IT   –   Engro

IT Recovery Team:

IT Recovery team primarily shall be responsible to:

- Review the action plan given in manual and to make necessary amendments if deemed necessary before its commencement.

- Review the project progress and to take necessary corrective actions.

The IT Recovery Team shall consist of the following individuals:

1. GM Finance   –   Team Leader

2. I & E Manager   – DHK   –   Member

3. Admin Manager   – KHI   –   Member

4. Admin Manager   – DHK   –   Member

5. IT Coordinator   –   Secretary

6. (IS Advisor shall be the IT Coordinator. His backup would be Systems Officer—DHK)

EXHIBIT 6 (CONTINUED)

CASES IN MANAGEMENT PRACTICES 141

MIDAS Recovery:

1. MIDAS shall be available at recovery site (DHK) only, therefore, all key users from KHI and regional offices shall move to DHK.

2. Each regional office (except DHK) shall send one Office Assistant to recovery site to do all the data entry for his region.

3. As soon as MIDAS is available to users at recovery site, they will run the relevant reports from the list in Appendix II to find out the last document entered in the system. All missing documents will have to be re-entered.

4. Regional office shall send all the documents (such as Customer orders, PER, PDAs, Payment Instruments—DDs etc) to the recovery site at DHK.

5. Required MIDAS reports shall be either faxed or couriered to regional office.

The MIDAS Recovery Team shall be responsible to start the MIDAS related operations as quickly as possible.

SAP Recovery:

One server for SAP recovery has been placed at plant site—DHK. Complete backup of SAP server in head office is sent to DHK on tape cartridge on weekly basis (Every Monday).

In order to give the latest data to the SAP users, the SAP data from the weekly tape cartridge (at DHK) shall be uploaded to the SAP recovery server. SAP client shall be installed on PCs to enable the access to SAP recovery servers.

All SAP users shall run the relevant reports to find out the last document/vouchers (such as vendor payment etc) available in the system.

Source: Company records.

2.2 PAK ARAB REFINERY LIMITED (PARCO)— MANAGEMENT OF CIRCULAR DEBT

CASE HIGHLIGHTS AND KEY POINTS

The case is about how a very large intra corporate debt was built up in the Pakistan economy among private and public sector energy companies in 2009. It deals with both the micro decisions regarding trade debtors at the corporate level by PARCO as well as their macroeconomic impact when the debt was viewed on a national level and called circular debt. The energy and power sectors are discussed in the case, along with the reasons for the circular debt. The government was heavily involved in regulating the power sector and had not resolved the issue of reimbursement of targetted subsidy on a timely basis, nor did it show any eagerness to ask large Public Sector Enterprises (PSEs) such as Pakistan International Airlines (PIA) to pay their power bills. The main focus is on how to resolve the very large amounts of debt that had accumulated in various energy companies. The Government of Pakistan through the Ministry of Petroleum and Natural Resources (MP&NR) was closely involved in the oil sector either by holding majority shares in oil companies or through regulation. A secondary analysis can look at the impact of regulation on the operations of oil companies.

The case can be used in a number of subject areas such as:

Management control: to evaluate working capital debt problems, risk management of the foreign exchange (FX) risks, use of currency swaps to reduce this risk, cash flow fluctuation, and the regulatory risks. Ratio analysis can be done on the financial performance data in the exhibits.

Corporate governance: to examine the role of the directors and managers of Pakistan State Oil (PSO), which was controlled by the Government, in dealing with the Ministry of Petroleum and Natural Resources.

Business government relations: to enable the company to convince the government officials that the changes made in setting the pricing and other regulations were detrimental to the oil business.

There were direct controls being exercised by Government of Pakistan via the oil price setting mechanism and the indirect affect via the circular debt that would, in normal circumstances, be the domain of the directors and management of the companies.

LEVEL OF ANALYSIS FOR WHICH THE CASE HAS BEEN WRITTEN

This case is intended to test a student's:

1. Understanding of complex oil business operations, especially the working capital arrangements.

2. Ability to gather related facts spread out within the case and link them coherently from a financial analyst point of view.

3. Basic understanding of financial analysis and understanding the role of the government in current economic conditions.

4. Understanding the supply chain.

This case requires the student to have a good understanding of how the working capital items were inter-related. The receivables of PARCO had blocked funds of the company as the payments had not been received on time and this had an impact on payables of PARCO. The behavior of payables will normally mimic that of the receivables. If the working capital was not managed properly this could cause the company to choke and go down as without cash there is no life in the business. There are two years of summarized financials in the case that have deteriorating asset ratios such as days receivable.

The students will require sound business knowledge obtained through either work experience or after having completed the first year of an MBA program. They will need to understand the regulatory framework of an organization and how organizations operate with the constraints imposed by the framework.

ASSIGNMENT QUESTIONS

Questions:

1. Prepare a draft of the report for Mr Hameed which he can present at the meeting in Dubai. (list of points is acceptable.)

2. What method of collecting problem receivables are normally employed and what were the factors preventing PARCO from collecting its receivable from PSO in the usual manner?

3. What is a circular debt and what causes it to be called circular, How could the

commercial banks or any other organization help to resolve this crises? What steps should the government take?

4. Are TFCs the only way that the debt can be paid? If there is an alternative please explain your answer.

5. What are the risks facing PARCO due to fluctuations in oil price, foreign exchange movements, delayed payment of receivables?

6. Discuss the strategic importance of an oil company to an economy?

7. How do regulations impact the operations of the oil company?

CASE TEXT: PAK ARAB REFINERY LIMITED (PARCO)— MANAGEMENT OF CIRCULAR DEBT

Introduction

On 21 October 2009, Amar Hameed, the chief financial officer of Pak Arab Refinery Limited (PARCO), was preparing to travel from Karachi, Pakistan to the quarterly management meeting in Abu Dhabi, in the United Arab Emirates. Hameed had been asked by the managing director to write a detailed report on the circumstances, the stakeholders involved, and the reasons that had led to the buildup of PARCO's huge debt. In the previous management meeting, the managing director had warned the directors that payment of the letter of credit for the latest crude shipment due to be received on 14 November, had to be made in the fourth quarter, but PARCO's ability to make the payment would be in jeopardy if the money it was owed from Pakistan State Oil (PSO) was not received by that date. The unaudited results of 30 September 2009 showed that the debt due from PSO had increased to almost Rs. 26 billion[1] (US$300 million). The newspapers were full of reports that the national inter-corporate debt had reached a crisis level and that the government had not been taking timely action as the issue involved large government-owned enterprises.

---

1 During 2009, the average rate of exchange between the U.S. dollar and the Pakistan rupee was US$1 = PKR82.

PAKISTAN ENERGY SECTOR

Oil Sector

The Government of Pakistan, through the Ministry of Petroleum and Natural Resources (MP&NR), was closely involved in the oil sector, both by holding majority shares in oil companies and through regulation. As the Pakistan economy grew during the 1960s, the multinational oil companies, such as Shell, Exxon, and Caltex started operations locally. While at the inception, some of these companies operated as fully owned and controlled subsidiaries of foreign shareholders, by 2009, the economic scenario had changed. In the mid-1970s, a policy was introduced to nationalize many of the large businesses, which, subsequently was followed by a policy reversal and a large number of privatizations in the 1990s. The oil sector thus was a mix of government regulated and market-oriented organizations.

Pakistan had established the government-owned Oil and Gas Development Corporation (OGDC), which was engaged in oil exploration and development of new sources of energy. The local oil production in 2009 was approximately 65,000 barrels per day (bpd), whereas the demand was 359,000 bpd.[2] The MP&NR had developed plans to enhance the domestic oil output as the oil price reached a very high level, causing the import bill to rise, which then led to huge trade deficits and a decline in the value of the rupee against the U.S. dollar. In 2009, the total demand for petrol, oil and lubricants (POL) products had not changed substantially from 2008, as the economy reacted to the global financial crises. The transportation sector was the highest consumer of POL products, followed by the power generation sector.

The total consumption of POL products in 2008/09 in Pakistan was 18.74 million tons. The total refinery output in Pakistan was 8.87 million tons, and 9.85 million tons of petroleum products had been imported. POL products were a major component of Pakistan's annual imports; however, because of the rise in the price of oil, there was a pressing need to expand exploration and to seek new local sources of oil and gas. The oil marketing companies (OMCs) and refineries were allowed to import 5.1 million metric tons (mmt) of

---

2   Oil Companies Advisory Committee (OCAC).

furnace oil (FO) and 4.3 mmt of high-speed diesel (HSD) during the year.[3] In this regard, government and the OGDC had made plans to expand the refining sector and to invest in new exploration. Recently the OGDC had granted licenses for oil exploration and the Oil & Gas Regulatory Agency (OGRA) had approved the setting up of two new refineries.

Pak Arab Refinery Limited (PARCO)

The Pak Arab Refinery was a fully integrated energy company which had been set up as a public limited company (although not listed on the Karachi Stock Exchange) to undertake the joint venture between the governments of the Emirate of Abu Dhabi and Pakistan. The shareholding was 60 per cent by the government of Pakistan and 40 per cent by the emirate of Abu Dhabi. The company's mission was 'To maintain PARCO's flagship role in the country's energy sector by becoming a fully integrated oil conglomerate through broader vision, accentuated drive and professional excellence.[4]

PARCO operations consisted of oil refining and related activities, oil pipelines systems (see Exhibit 1), and storage facilities. The first milestone in its operational history[5] was in 1981, when the Karachi-Mahmood Kot (KMK) Crude-Cum-Product Pipeline System, which spanned more than 817 kilometres, started working. In 1994, the Bubak and Fazilpur pumping stations were set up, and the pumping capacity rose by 50 per cent to 6.0 million tons per year. Various pipeline extension projects were completed, extending the pipelines to Sheikupura via Faisalabad. A major project completed in 2000 was the start up of the 100,000 bpd Mid-Country Refinery (MCR) at Mahmood Kot.[6]

The company's investment in the pipeline infrastructure had helped to achieve an enhanced level of capability to supply more of the oil consumption needs of the Punjab province—the most populated of Pakistan's four provinces. Mahmood Kot refinery (see Exhibit 1) was well located. Within a 30-mile radius, two independent power plants (IPPs) were in production:

---

3   Pakistan State Oil working papers and Annual Report 2009.

4   Pak Arab Refinery Limited, 'Vision & Mission', www.parco.com.pk/index.php?option=com_content&view=article&id=1
     63&Itemid=224, accessed 18 February 2011.

5   Pak Arab Refinery Limited, 'Growth and Performance', www.parco.com.pk/index.php?option=com_content&view=articl
     e&id=175&Itemid=231, accessed 18 February 2011.

6   Ibid.

KAPCO, producing approximately 1,500 megawatts (MW), and AES Powergen, producing approximately 725 MW. More IPPs were being set up. The company was the largest among the five refineries whose financial summaries and production capacities are shown in Exhibit 2 and Exhibit 3.

PARCO also had strategic partnerships with Total PARCO Pakistan Ltd. (TPPL), SHV Energy Pakistan, and OMV.

Total PARCO Pakistan Ltd. (TPPL)

TPPL was a joint venture between PARCO and TOTAL S.A of France. TPPL was marketing consumer petroleum products through its national network of retail outlets. In 2009, TPPL had more than 175 retail outlets around the country.[7]

SHV Energy Pakistan

SHV of Holland was marketing 25 per cent of PARCO's LPG [liquefied petroleum gas] production as 'PEARL Gas' under a Technical Services & Support Agreement (TSSA). SHV Holdings N.V is a Fortune 500 multinational operating in FMCG [fast moving consumer goods] warehousing, natural gas exploration, venture capital, and LPG [liquefied petroleum gas] marketing and distribution, with a presence in more than 36 countries. The SHV Gas Division operated in the downstream LPG marketing and distribution business and specialized in providing an economical, efficient, and complete energy solution to industrial, commercial, and domestic users.[8]

OMV

PARCO also marketed lubricants all over Pakistan in association with OMV, Austria. OMV, an oil and gas company, engaged in the exploration, production, refining,

---

7   Pak Arab Refinery Limited, 'Joint Venture (JV) Partners', http://www.parco.com.pk/index.php?option=com_content&view=article&id=174&Itemid=230, accessed 5 March 2011.

8   Ibid.

transportation, and marketing of oil and gas. It had petrochemical properties in Austria, Kazakhstan, Libya, New Zealand, Pakistan, Romania, Tunisia, the United Kingdom, and Central and Eastern Europe. OMV is headquartered in Vienna, Austria.

Oil Marketing Companies (OMCs)

The oil marketing companies (OMCs) consisted of three major companies: Chevron (formerly Caltex), Shell, and Pakistan State Oil (PSO). PSO was far larger than the others and dominated this sector. It was controlled by the government, with a 51 per cent shareholding and was in the business of providing its customers with fuel for transportation, energy for heat and light, retail services, and petrochemicals products for industrial and individual needs all over the country. The key fuel products dealt with by PSO along with market share are shown in Exhibit 4. In 2008/09, PSO had an annual sales turnover of Rs. 700 billion (US$8.5 billion) (see Exhibit 5).

In 2008/09, the overall consumption of POL products had remained almost unchanged from the previous year, and the negligible increases in consumption of Mogas and JP1 were more than offset by the decreases in diesel and SKO.

In Pakistan, the sale of POL products was a huge business, in which PSO had 70 per cent of the share of the sales. Accordingly, the delay in receiving payments, due to the circular debt, had made a big impact on PSO's results (see Exhibit 5). The results in 2008/09 showed that as at 30 June 2009, the payables to the refineries and foreign oil suppliers had increased by Rs. 25 billion to Rs. 96 billion as compared to the previous year.

Power Sector

The country as a whole was facing a shortage of electricity, and as a significant amount of power was generated using POL products, the fuel supplied by PSO needed to remain uninterrupted.

Pakistan had five main electric power producers. They and their installed capacities are shown below.[9]

Power Producer	Installed Capacity (in MW)	% of Total Production
Water and Power Development Authority (WAPDA)	6461	33
Pakistan Electric Power Company (Pvt) Limited (PEPCO)	4811	24
Karachi Electric Supply Company (KESC)	1756	9
Pakistan Atomic Energy Commission (PAEC)	462	2
Independent Power Producers (IPPs)	6365	32
Total	19855	100

Water and Power Development Authority (WAPDA)

WAPDA was established in 1958 as a semi-autonomous government agency to coordinate the development of Pakistan's water and power resources. Over the years, WAPDA's span of activities grew under its two parts called the Water Wing and the Power Wing. The Power Wing was responsible for the planning, construction, and operation of power generators, transmission, and distribution facilities throughout the country, except the Karachi area, which was served by KESC. As the size of WAPDA Power Wing grew the free market economic doctrine adopted by the government led to the corporatization of this wing.

The privatization efforts of the power sector that commenced in 2008 had resulted in a hive off[10] WAPDA, which was left with a role much smaller than before. Its new role was to exclusively focus on hydroelectric power and develop dams or lakes as the new water sources.

Pakistan Electricity Power Company (Pvt) Limited (PEPCO)

The WAPDA Act was amended in 1998 and the work of the Power wing was split into a new company. Pakistan Electricity Power Company (Pvt) Limited (PEPCO) had been set

---

9   www.forum.noorclinic.com/thread.php?topic=19335, accessed 30 April 2011.

10   To hive off means to separate one part of a company, usually by selling it. Cambridge Dictionaries Online, http://dictionary.cambridge.org/dictionary/british/hive-sth-off, accessed 22 May 2011.

up as a holding company to manage the remaining, mainly non-hydroelectric generation of power. PEPCO had 14 subsidiaries:

- Four (4) thermal power generation companies (GENCOs)

- One (1) National Transmission & Power Dispatch Company (NTDC)

- Nine (9) distribution companies (DISCOs)

Each company was registered under the company law in Pakistan and had a board of directors. Although each company performed its main function independently, PEPCO was closely involved in dealings with the government and any issue that was common to all companies. In order to establish good governance practices, the board of each of the subsidiaries included private-sector individuals and company employees.

Karachi Electricity Supply Company (KESC)

Karachi Electricity Supply Company (KESC) was involved with both generating power and supplying it to consumers in and around the industrial and commercial port city of Karachi. The company owned 1,750 MW of generation capacity (oil- and gas-fired) of which 1,530 MW was operational. The approximate demand for power in Karachi was 2,300 MW per day. To meet the supply-demand gap, KESC purchased power from PEPCO, WAPDA, and independent power producers (IPPs), such as the Hub Power Company Limited (HUBCO). Their transmission and generation equipment was very old, so frequent breakdowns were normal. If a shortfall occurred in the supply of power by the external plants, the company resorted to, 'load shedding,' which referred to scheduled power shutdowns, but cuts could occur at any time. A very high amount of energy was lost in transmission (line losses accounted for 15 to 20 per cent of the power available to KESC for supply), which was causing serious revenue shortfalls.

Pakistan Atomic Energy Commission

Pakistan Atomic Energy Commission (PAEC) was a government organization doing research in nuclear technology. PAEC also operated two power plants.

Independent Power Producers

Numerous independent power producers (IPPs) had been established after 1991. The IPPs generated power but they sold it in bulk to PEPCO, WAPDA, or to KESC. These power plants used furnace oil, diesel, or gas for generating electricity. One of the larger IPPs in the private sector was the Hub Power Company Limited (HUBCO), which had an installed generation capacity of 1,200 MW. HUBCO was incorporated in Pakistan in 1991 and was a publicly owned company listed on Pakistan's three stock exchanges. Its principal activity had been to own, operate, and maintain an oil-fired thermal power plant, which provided approximately six per cent of the total electricity generated in the country. The HUBCO power station was the first and largest power station financed by the private sector in South Asia. Pakistan's shortage in power gave HUBCO the opportunity to expand its operations and had led to the planning of two new projects: a 220 MW thermal power project and an 84 MW hydroelectric project located downstream of one of the dams.[11]

The Circular Debt

Pakistan's circular debt was mainly prevailing among departments or companies owned or controlled by the government. The key players in the energy sector, which were involved in the creation of or were affected by the very large amount of inter-corporate debt, also called 'circular debt,' are shown in Exhibit 6. The distributors looked after the billing and collection of the charges related to power supplied but PEPCO, as the holding company, was responsible when any billing- or collection-related issues arose. The sources of receipts and the areas of payments that were involved are shown in Exhibit 7.

Buildup of Circular Debt

The inter-corporate circular debt arose in one of two ways:

1. The distribution company, KESC, often failed to collect bills from all of its consumers. KESC also incurred very high line losses during distribution, consequently, the

---

11 Hubco Annual Report, 2009.

payment it received was inadequate to meet its cash needs. Some large government-owned corporations, such as Pakistan International Airlines (PIA), did not pay, causing KESC to default on payments to power producers (e.g. an IPP). PIA was also affected by the steep and sudden rise in fuel prices in 2008 and as a result had a negative equity of Rs. 47.5 billion (US$ 580 million) on 31 December 2008. The power plants' receivables were not liquidated, so they were not able to make payments for fuel oil purchases from the distributor PSO, which in turn delayed settling the payables to refineries. This recurrent problem caused a chain of cash-flow shortfalls in all energy companies, which needed to borrow from banks to meet their expenditures, thereby incurring a high cost of borrowing. The movement of funds among the various stakeholders is shown in Exhibit 7. The relationships were so tight that if one link were to be disrupted, the whole process chain would be affected.

2. Another reason for the increase in inter-corporate circular debt was that the circular debt had been accumulating since 2008, when the government had provided a tariff subsidy as the oil prices per barrel rose to a high of approximately US$140 (see Exhibit 8). The government, in view of political constraints, decided to give an all-time high subsidy on high-speed diesel (HSD), which was used mainly by the transport sector. As a result, in June 2008, the government paid a highest ever subsidy of PKR 37.07 (US$0.46) per liter on diesel, which amounted to PKR 30 billion (US$375 million) per month. The price increase required at the gasoline stations would have caused a sudden steep rise in diesel price, which could have triggered hyperinflation, as Pakistan's domestic inflation was already very high. The differential between the price charged to the consumer and the international price paid to the producer or refinery was reimbursable to PSO/PARCO refinery as price differential claim (PDC). This tariff subsidy was claimed as PDC by PSO from the MP&NR (see Exhibit 9) and PSO had a long waiting period to recover this subsidy in cash from the government, which meant that PSO had to borrow to meet its business needs. The government had agreed with its international lenders that the tariff subsidies would be phased out by 30 June 2009.

A senior economist and former chief economist of the Government of Pakistan, Ashfaque Hasan, said:

The inefficient electricity supply and distribution system in the country also contributed to the problem. The theft of power was rampant in many cities, and this was a key element in the line losses, something that scarred the financial health of power utilities.[12]

Effect of the Debt

The State Bank of Pakistan report for 2008/09 stated the effect of the circular debt as follows:

As the circular debt situation unfolded in FY09, this had two significant implications:

1. **Contraction in industrial productivity in a number of industries as energy slippages intensified.** The liquidity constraints in refineries and OMCs, resulted mainly from circular debt issue, did not allow them to import sufficient crude oil necessary to operate at their usual capacity. As a result, a number of refineries and power industries were forced to produce below capacity throughout the year.

2. **High banks' exposure on energy and power entities as demand for banks' finance increased**. The delays in the settlement of differential claims with government and the utilities forced some of the corporations to obtain short-term bridge finance from banks. Thus, demand for banks finance increased drastically during early months of FY09. This has not only caused immense pressures on banks' liquidity but also increased banks' exposures to these entities. As the magnitude of exposure got close to the prescribed limits, some banks became reluctant to extend incremental loans to these entities in H2-FY09.[13]

Government Actions

The government action plan was included in the budget speech for fiscal year 2009/10, presented on 14 June 2009, by the Minister for Finance Hina Rabbani Khar:

---

12 Inter-corporate circular debt balloons; Tuesday, 10 November 2009 09:57 Courtesy: The News, http://www.forexpk.com/highlights/business-news/inter-corporate-circular-debt-balloons.html, accessed 18 February 2011.

13 State Bank of Pakistan Annual Report 2008-2009 Pages 86 and 87.

In order to improve the liquidity position of the power sector, the Government specially-created holding company will assume the entire bank loan liabilities of Rs. 216 billion and pay the markup on these loans from budgetary resources; has already arranged TFC facilities of Rs. 92 billion for PEPCO from banks to discharge its payment obligations towards Independent Power Producers and oil and gas companies; will assist to settle the remaining payables of PEPCO at Rs. 61 billion; has decided to pick up the entire past arrears of PEPCO against FATA [Federally Administered Tribal Areas] consumers to the tune of Rs. 80 billion and pay the current electricity bill of FATA; and will help PEPCO to clear its outstanding receivables from federal and provincial government departments and entities, mainly KESC and KW&SB.[14] Projects have been undertaken to reinforce the transmission and distribution systems to minimize power losses and outages so as to provide a stable and reliable supply to consumers.[15]

To meet the working capital needs caused by unpaid tariff subsidy claims and nonpayment of power bills by large government customers, PEPCO had been borrowing on behalf of its subsidiaries from the banking system against government guarantees. As stated in the budget speech in June 2009, the government had set up a special purpose company—Power Holding Company (Pvt) Limited—and had started the process to transfer Rs. 216 billion to this company.

On 30 September 2009, PHCL issued Rs. 85 billion term finance certificates (TFCs)[16] backed by a government guarantee. The TFCs, which had a maturity period of five years, were priced at Karachi Inter Bank Offer Rate (KIBOR)[17] plus 200 basis points but were not traded. This was the second issue of TFC: in March, TFCs amounting to Rs. 80 billion were issued by PEPCO at 175 basis points above KIBOR. The government plan to complete the transfer of the debt by 31 March 2009 was delayed due to stringent conditions being laid down by the commercial banks that had lent money to the PEPCO subsidiaries. The 2008/09 annual report on the economy by the State Bank of Pakistan (SBP) had

---

14 KWSB = Karachi Water and Sewage Board.

15 'Pakistan Budget Speech for Fiscal Year 2000–2010,' www.maybenow.com/PAKISTAN-BUDGET-SPEECH-FOR-FISCAL-YEAR-2009-2010-q23972778, accessed 2 February 2011.

16 Term Finance Certificates = TFCs. These were debt instruments in the form of cash deposit receipts and accrued interest payments on a fixed or variable rate basis for a predetermined period.

17 On 30 September 2009, the bid/offer Karachi Interbank Offer rate (KIBOR) for 3-year tenor was 12.91 / 13.47%, as per the State Bank of Pakistan.

mentioned that the loans extended to the power sector in the financial year 2008/09 were concentrated in the top five banks and that, as the banks' exposure in the power sector was already sizeable and growing further, banks were reluctant to finance any new project in the power sector.

Oil Sector Debt

The five refineries in the country were all facing financial crises as their receivables were not converting into cash, which affected their production plans. Most of the refineries had fully utilized their lines of credit made available by the commercial banks. PARCO's financial expenses had more than doubled in 2009 to Rs. 10.3 billion, from Rs. 4.9 billion in 2008. This increase in expenses was accompanied by a reduction in sales from Rs. 198 billion in 2008 to Rs. 173 billion in 2009. As a result, the company reported a sharp drop in its profits, down in 2009 to Rs. 5 billion from Rs. 15 billion in the year 2008.

The refineries had been incurring large losses on exchange and the cost of borrowing in rupees was also high (close to 14 per cent). To avoid similar losses in 2009, the Pakistan Refinery Limited (PRL) had approached the new multilateral trade financing bank—the Economic Cooperation Organization Trade & Development Bank—for a working capital loan. This new bank was formed by, among others, the governments of Pakistan, Turkey, and Iran to foster trade in the Economic Coordination Organization (ECO) region. A US$50 million trade finance facility was obtained to enable the purchase of crude oil. The company wanted U.S. dollar financing as its obligations under the letter of credit to suppliers were denominated in U.S. dollars, and the rates on U.S. dollar borrowing were in single digits so that the cost of the entire deal was low.[18]

The OMC, Pakistan State Oil Company also faced serious liquidity problems owing to increasing receivables from the IPPs, such as HUBCO, KAPCO, and the national airline PIA, which had defaulted on its payments to PSO. As of 30 June 2009, PSO's receivables from these entities stood at Rs. 80 billion (increase of Rs. 47 billion over 2008), which included Rs. 35 billion from HUBCO. Consequently, as PSO was short of cash, it had to delay payment to creditors and owed Rs. 96 billion (an increase of Rs. 27 billion over

---

18 Pakistan State Oil Annual Report, 2009.

2008) to local refineries, including Rs. 26 billion to PARCO, which also had resorted to short-term borrowings to remain in business. Due to the delay in receiving payment as a result of the circular debt, PSO had to incur unusually high financial expenses of Rs. 6.2 billion in FY09, compared with Rs. 1.3 billion in previous years.

PSO, as the major distributor of POL products, had also informed the government that its liquidity position did not allow it to guarantee the undisturbed supply of oil to the consumers. According to PSO management: 'We have already defaulted on our obligations to the local refineries which require advance payment for the supply of products which is further aggravating the company's liquidity crunch.'[19]

The country's oil sector was facing a situation with no prompt resolution in sight. As a result, the two major stakeholders, PARCO and PSO, jointly informed the MP&NR of the consequences of not resolving the circular debt issue. They explained that as the major amount of annual consumption was based on imported oil, the two companies would face problems in opening letters of credit and thereby a shortage would result. They had also suggested to the government that funding be arranged for PSO earlier as its imports were more at risk. Exhibit 9 shows the receivables of the five refineries due from the government and PSO on 30 September 2009. Each refinery was keen to reduce the high cost of borrowing from the banks.

The press had reported that in order to impress the seriousness of the matter, the chief executive officers of all the five refineries had agreed to send a joint letter addressed to the Minister of MP&NR that the conditions were causing their businesses not to be viable:

> It must be realized that with no funds to procure crude supplies and each barrel of crude processed giving a net negative margin of US$3-6/barrel in case of most of the refineries, they cannot continue with their operations for an indefinite period.[20]

The Power Sector Debt

The companies directly affected by the circular debt in the power sector were IPPs

---

19 Bhutta, 'Lingering Circular Debt Issue: PSO, Parco Warn Government of Massive Oil Crisis', Business Recorder, 10 September 2010.

20   Iqbal Mirza, 'Refineries on the Verge of Financial Collapse', Business Recorder, 23 November 2009.

who saw their receivables rise abnormally and as a result, their sales agreements with the customers were violated. The directors of the independent power project HUBCO commented in their quarterly report for the period ending 30 September 2009:

In its second tranche of the Circular Debt settlement of the WAPDA outstanding by the Government of Pakistan, HUBCO received a total amount of Rs. 28.4 billion of which Rs. 26.9 billion was immediately paid to PSO. Today an amount of Rs. 31 billion is outstanding against WAPDA and we in turn owe Rs. 29 billion to PSO. The WAPDA outstanding had also resulted in HUBCO having to maintain its Running Finance Facility at Rs. 7.5 billion.

Government Control in Oil Sector

The refineries' overall financial conditions and profitability had been seriously affected by the adverse changes made by the MP&NR in the pricing formula used to set product prices (see Exhibit 10) and the unfavorable fluctuations in the prices of petroleum products and crude oil. At Bosicor—the smallest of the refineries—earnings were seriously affected, leading to a loss of Rs. 10 billion posted for the year ended 30 June 2009. This loss included Rs. 440 million because of extra financial costs incurred directly due to the circular debt situation and a huge loss of Rs. 4.38 billion due to the fall of the rupee against the dollar on the foreign exchange markets (see Exhibit 11). Similarly, National Refinery Limited (NRL) faced a squeeze on its liquidity as the amounts receivable from PSO were delayed. The State Bank of Pakistan had not allowed oil companies to trade in currencies, which exposed the refineries to potential exchange losses. As result, NRL incurred a loss of Rs. 2.4 billion on payment of its oil import bills. Due to the rising parity between the Pakistan rupee and the U.S. dollar, Attock Refinery limited (ARL) also incurred a loss on exchange of Rs. 1,240 million during 2009 on crude purchases. A summary of the quarterly profit and loss results of the refineries (see Exhibit12) shows the variability in profits due to the regulations.

Refineries had highlighted that although the final recommendations made by the Ministry of Petroleum and Natural Resources (MP&NR) to the Economic Coordination Committee (ECC) in April 2009, would, to a certain extent, alleviate the negative profitability of the refineries, they would still not completely pull them out from a loss situation. Further, the government had also revised the pricing formula in August 2008 by reducing the duty on HSD from 10 per cent to 7.5 per cent and by revising the motor gasoline pricing mechanism to the disadvantage of the refineries. The chief executive officers (CEOs) had pointed out that the refineries' profitability (see Exhibit 12) during the last 15 months period had also been affected by the following two additional factors:

1. Foreign Exchange:

    In the monthly price determination by OGRA, the historical average of exchange rates prevailing in the previous months were applied to calculate the prices in Pak Rupees. However, in case of payments to crude oil suppliers, the exchange rate prevalent on the date of payment was used to calculate the amount payable in Pak Rupees as the SBP did not allow refineries to avail the forward exchange facility. The time lag between the rupees value on receipt of crude and value on date of payment resulted in a negative impact on the refineries. This was incorporated in the recommendations for revision of Pricing Formula.

2. Price determination period:

    The import parity prices for refineries, which were determined on a fortnightly basis, were changed to on a monthly basis in January 2009, whereas the crude oil pricing period in case of local supplies continued to be on weekly basis. This, again, had a negative impact on the refineries as in case of rising trend of crude prices [see Exhibit 8]. This was reflected in the products' prices with a time lag.[21]

To offset the negative impact arising from monthly determination of prices, the refiners had proposed that the petroleum products' price determination by OGRA should either be brought in line with the weekly crude prices mechanism or at least reverted to the fortnightly pricing basis. In 2006, the federal government had authorized OGRA to determine the price of gasoline in accordance with the prescribed formula. The federal government had also issued guidelines (see Exhibit 10) and parameters to enable calculation of the prices and had *inter alia* advised that the ex-factory and ex-depot prices would be set after approval by the federal government.

---

21 Ibid.

As Hameed prepared his notes for the meeting, he reflected on the following points: the circular debt was an issue whereby oil-marketing companies (OMCs), mainly PSO, had continuously defaulted on their payments to the refineries. The refineries had declared fluctuating results, which included losses in their quarterly financial results. They had been trying to explain to the officials of the MP&NR that changes in pricing formulae should not be so frequent. Hameed felt that numerous different variables were affecting the company's business and although many companies were involved, he would recommend to the PARCO management that they take a lead role and suggest to the other refineries what action they would like to be taken by the Ministry of Petroleum and Natural Resources.

PAK ARAB REFINERY LIMITED PIPELINE NETWORK IN PAKISTAN

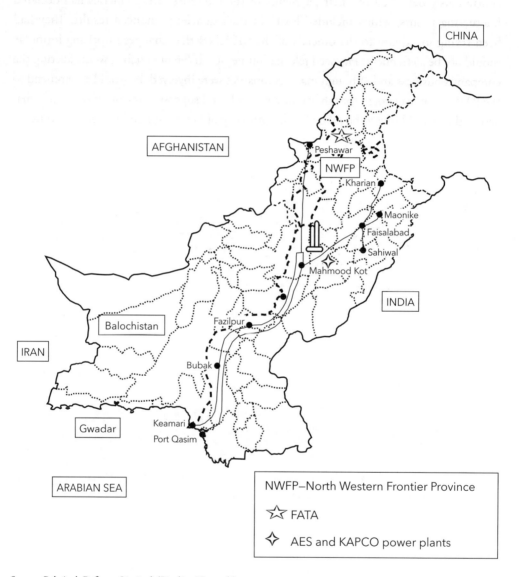

NWFP—North Western Frontier Province

☆ FATA

✧ AES and KAPCO power plants

Source: Pak Arab Refinery Limited, 'Pipeline Network'.
www.parco.com.pk/index.php?option=com_content&view=article&id=190&Itemid=187, accessed 15 February 2011.
Provinces and neighboring countries added by case writer.

EXHIBIT 2

CASES IN MANAGEMENT PRACTICES 163

FINANCIAL SUMMARY OF REFINERIES IN PAKISTAN FOR 2008 AND 2009

COMPANY	BOSICOR Refinery Limited		Attock Refinery Limited		Pakistan Refinery Limited		National Refinery Limited		Pak Arab Oil Refinery Limited	
Year	2009	2008	2009	2008	2009	2008	2009	2008	2009	2008
Net Revenue (in Rs millions)	44,621	35,806	77,260	93,654	76,861	57,404	109,578	129,386	173,798	198,658
Gross Profit	(3,909)	2,142	1,918	4,008	(3,013)	4,775	5,273	10,681	9,605	30,275
Operating (Loss)/Profit	(4,504)	1,762	79	2,309	(3,038)	3,843	5,207	10,163	4,355	25,958
Financial Costs including FX Loss	6,160	506	1,471	1,244	2,477	–	2,394	–	10,289	4,956
(Loss)/Profit before Tax	(10,327)	184	1,072	2,887	–	3,255	2,813	8,831	5,783	23,458
(Loss)/Profit after Tax	(10,333)	15	406	2,007	(4,571)	2,111	1,533	6,005	5,360	15,244
EBITDA)	685	–	2,653	–	(4,762)	3,631	5,442	–	7,291	28,806
Balance Sheet										
Share Capital	3,921	3,921	852	711	360	350	800	800	11,605	11,605
Reserves	(6,512)	8	9,294	8,988	1,829	6,455	16,553	16,619	32,502	37,156
Shareholders' Equity	(2,591)	3,529	10,146	9,699	2,189	6,805	17,353	17,419	44,107	48,761
Property Plant & Equipment	14,778	8,565	2,916	2,929	2,343	990	3,019	2,032	32,760	34,244
Long-Term Investment	95	–	13,440	13,135	1,078	–	169	–	5,376	9,343
Net Current Assets	(6,385)	(2,152)	(4,167)	(4,578)	(1,229)	5,767	14,300	14,874	16,315	18,141
Long-Term Liabilities	11,079	1,369	120	97	4	47	135	312	14,142	16,530
Profitability Ratios										
Gross Profit Ratio (%)	−8.76	5.98	2.48	4.28	−3.92	5.00	4.81	8.26	5.53	15.24

Net Profit Ratio (%)	−23.16	0.04	−0.73	2.14	−5.95	2.20	1.40	4.64	3.08	7.67
EBITDA Margin (%)	–	–	–	–	−6.20	3.80	–	–	4.20	14.50
Return on Shareholders' Equity (%)	398.80	0.43	4.00	22.33	−208.82	31.00	8.83	34.47	12.15	31.26
Asset Utilization										
Inventory Turnover Ratio (in days)	11.30	4.45	13.50	–	9.00	28.60	8.17	11.32	36.33	27.90
Debtor Turnover Ratio (in days)	4.91	11.30	8.00	–	6.14	13.40	41.09	22.68	63.16	36.32
Fixed Asset Turnover Ratio (in days)	4.18	4.18	76.37	–	3.05	123.10	53.28	63.30	5.31	5.80

Source: extracted by the author from company Annual Reports or provided by the company (PARCO) for the respective years.

EXHIBIT 3

CASES IN MANAGEMENT PRACTICES 165

OWNERSHIP AND CAPACITY OF REFINERIES IN PAKISTAN

Name	Ownership	Capacity in Barrels per Day	Capacity in Millions of Tons
BOSICOR Refinery Limited	Public unlisted	30,000	1.5
Attock Refinery Limited	26% government owned	40,000	1.8
Pakistan Refinery Limited	Public	50,000	2.2
National Refinery Limited	Privatized; owned by Attock Group	65,000	2.8
Pak Arab Oil Refinery Limited	60% government owned	100,000	4.5
Total		285,000	12.8

Source: Company Annual Reports, 2009.

EXHIBIT 4

PAKISTAN STATE OIL STATISTICS, 2008/09

Main Petrol, Oil and Lubricants Products	Sales (in millions of tons)	Market share %
HSD (Diesel)	4.67	61
Mogas (Gasoline)	0.73	48
JP1 (Jet fuel)	0.41	66
SKO	0.10	56
FO (Furnace oil)	6.98	86
LDO	0.03	32

Note: HSD = high-speed diesel; SKO = Superior Kerosene Oil; LDO = Light Diesel Oil
Source: Pakistan State Oil Annual Report, 2009.

EXHIBIT 5

CASES IN MANAGEMENT PRACTICES 167

PAKISTAN STATE OIL FINANCIAL SUMMARY, 2004 TO 2009

Year		2009	2008	2007	2006	2005	2004
Sales Volume (in Millions of Tons)		13.2	13	11.8	9.8	9.7	8.6
Profit & Loss Account							**Rs in millions**
Sales Revenue		719,282	583,214	411,058	352,515	253,777	195,130
Net Revenue		612,696	495,279	349,706	298,250	212,504	161,538
Gross Profit		3,010	30,024	12,259	17,207	13,746	9,191
Operating (Loss)/Profit		(5,577)	22,451	7,950	11,264	9,340	6,452
Marketing & Admin. Expenses		5,113	4,425	3,748	3,428	3,219	2,634
(Loss)/Profit before Tax		(11,357)	21,377	7,122	11,418	9,191	6,263
(Loss)/Profit after Tax		(6,699)	14,054	4,690	7,525	5,656	4,212
Balance Sheet							
Share Capital		1,715	1,715	1,715	1,715	1,715	1,715
Reserves		19,156	29,250	19,224	19,098	15,830	13,731
Shareholders' Equity		20,871	30,965	20,939	20,813	17,545	15,446
Property Plant & Equipment		7,056	7,567	8,138	7,674	8,256	7,738
Net Current Assets		8,666	22,143	11,128	10,978	7,970	6,309
Long-Term Liabilities		2,528	2,409	2,412	2,299	1,999	1,636
Profitability Ratios							
Gross Profit Ratio	%	0.42	5.15	2.98	4.88	5.42	4.71
Net Profit Ratio	%	(0.93)	2.41	1.14	2.13	2.23	2.16
EBITDA Margin	%	(0.55)	4.10	2.29	3.80	4.16	3.71
Return on Shareholders' Equity	%	(32.10)	45.39	22.40	36.16	32.24	27.27
Return on Total Assets	%	(4.37)	11.06	6.28	10.72	10.81	9.93
Return on Capital Employed	%	15.50	68.10	35.40	54.10	48.90	40.80
Asset Utilization							
Inventory Turnover Ratio	(x)	13.90	10.10	11.70	11.50	11.20	13.10
Debtor Turnover Ratio	(x)	12.60	24.60	32.50	38.10	39.90	40.10
Creditor Turnover Ratio	(x)	6.30	9.60	10.80	12.50	13.50	12.20

Total Asset Turnover Ratio	(x)	5.13	5.78	5.67	5.76	5.36	5.22
Fixed Asset Turnover Ratio	(x)	98.40	74.30	52.00	44.30	31.70	27.50
Leverage							
Debt: Equity Ratio		–	–	–	–	–	–
Interest Cover Ratio	(x)	–	16.40	6.90	12.70	25.20	34.10
Current Ratio		1.07	1.24	1.22	1.23	1.24	1.25
Quick Ratio	(x)	0.75	0.57	0.64	0.63	0.62	0.66

Source: Pakistan State Oil Annual Reports.

EXHIBIT 6

CASES IN MANAGEMENT PRACTICES 169

KEY PLAYERS IN PAKISTAN'S ENERGY SECTOR

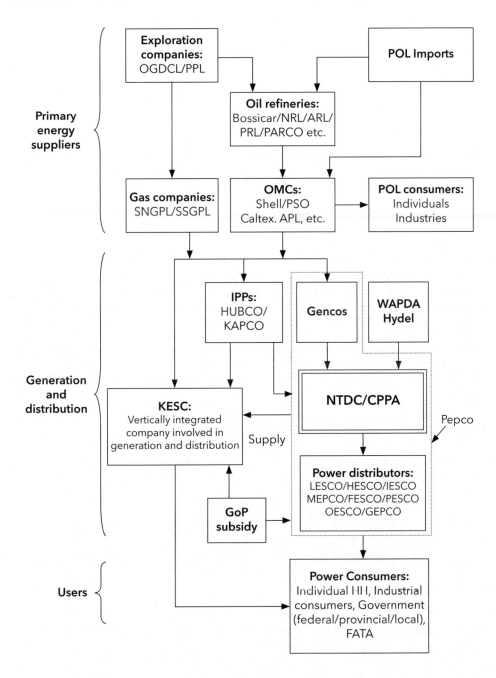

EXHIBIT 6 (CONTINUED)

Summary of Key Players

Category	Organizations
Fuel suppliers	PSO, PARCO
Power distributors	KESC (also a generator), PEPCO subsidiaries
Independent power producers	HUBCO, KAPCO
PEPCO as holding company managed various distribution companies	Distribution companies: e.g., LESCO,GESCO, National Transmission and Dispatch Company
Government departments (provincial and federal)	Pakistan International Airlines, Pakistan Railways
Ministry of Petroleum & Natural Affairs	Payment of subsidy (PDC)

Note: OGDCL = Oil and Gas Development Company; PPL = Pakistan Petroleum Limited; NRL = National Refinery Limited; ARL = Attock Refinery Limited; PRL = Pakistan Refinery Limited; PARCO = Pak Arab Oil Refinery Limited; POL = Petrol, Oil, and Lubricants; SNGPL = Sui Northern Gas Pipelines Limited; SSGPL = Sui Southern Gas Pipelines Limited; PSO = Pakistan State Oil; IPPs = Independent Power Plants; HUBCO = Hub Power Company Limited; KAPCO = Kot Addu Power Company Limited; Gencos = Thermal Power Generation Companies; WAPDA = Water and Power Development Authority; KESC = Karachi Electricity Supply Company; NTDC = National Transmission & Power Dispatch Company; CPPA = Unknown; PEPCO = Pakistan Electric Power Company (Pvt) Limited; LESCO = Lahore Electric Supply Company Limited; HESCO = Hyderabad Electric Supply Company; IESCO = Islamabad Electric Supply Company Limited: MEPCO = Multan Electric Power Company; FESCO = Faisalabad Electric; PESCO = Peshawar Electric; OESCO = Unknown; GEPCO = Gujranwala Electric Power Company; GoP = Government of Pakistan; HH = Household; FATA = Federally Administered Tribal Areas; APL = Attock Petroleum Limited; GESCO = Gujranwala Electric Supply Company; PDC = Price Differential Claim.

Source: Syed Sajid Ali and Sadia Badar, 'Dynamics of Circular Debt in Pakistan and its Resolution', *The Lahore Journal of Economics*, 15 September 2010, pp. 61–74.

EXHIBIT 7

CASES IN MANAGEMENT PRACTICES 171

FLOW OF RECEIPTS AND PAYMENTS IN PAKISTAN'S ENERGY SECTOR

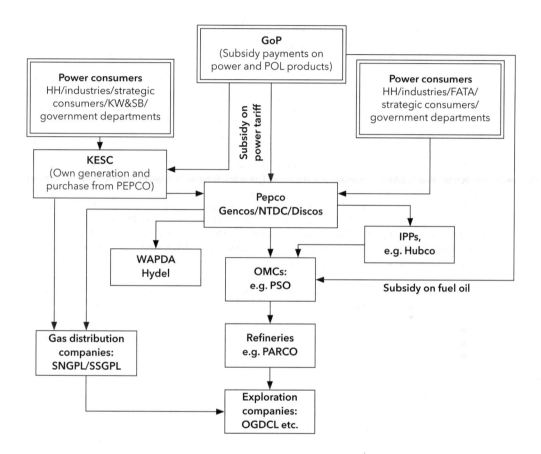

EXHIBIT 7 (CONTINUED)

Summary of Flows

Receipts	Payments
Utility bills collected from:	To suppliers
• Large Government organizations: e.g., the national police, national airline PIA, railways	• Oil Marketing Companies: e.g., PSO
• Private consumers	• Gas companies
• KESC which was a customer of PEPCO	Power generators: e.g., the IPP called HUBCO
Government tariff subsidy on certain category of consumers, price differential claim.	

Note: GoP = Government of Pakistan; POL = Petroleum, Oil, and Lubricants; HH = Unknown; KW&SB = Karachi Water and Sewage Board; FATA = Federally Administered Tribal Areas; KESC = Karachi Electric Supply Company; PEPCO = Pakistan Electric Power Company (Pvt) Limited; Gencos = Thermal Power Generation Companies; NTDC = National Transmission & Power Dispatch Company; Discos = Distribution Companies; WAPDA = Water and Power Development Authority; OMCs = Oil Marketing Companies; PSO = Pakistan State Oil; IPPs = Independent Power Producers; SNGPL = Sui Northern Gas Pipelines Limited; SSGPL = Sui Southern Gas Pipelines Limited; PARCO = Pak Arab Refinery Limited; OGDCL = Oil and Gas Development Company Limited; PIA = Pakistan International Airlines; HUBCO = Hub Power Company Limited.

Source: Sayed Sajid Ali and Sadia Badar, 'Dynamics of Circular Debt in Pakistan and its Resolution', *The Lahore Journal of Economics*, 15 September 2010, pp. 61–74.

EXHIBIT 8

CASES IN MANAGEMENT PRACTICES 173

OIL PRICES, 2002/03 TO 2008/09

Daily Arabian Light Crude Closing Prices per Barrel

July–June	Highest Quote (in US$)	Lowest Quote (in US$)	Average Daily Close (in US$)	Year-on-Year Change of Average Daily Close %
2002/03	33.10	22.60	27.20	–
2003/04	37.70	24.90	30.20	11.0%
2004/05	55.00	32.50	41.20	36.4%
2005/06	69.90	49.90	58.70	42.5%
2006/07	73.80	48.50	61.20	4.3%
2007/08	140.60	66.10	92.60	51.3%
2008/09	143.60	32.70	67.10	−27.5%

Source: State Bank of Pakistan Annual Report, 2008–09.

EXHIBIT 9

RECEIVABLES OF PAKISTAN'S OIL REFINERIES FROM PAKISTAN STATE OIL AND GOVERNMENT, AS ON 30 SEPTEMBER 2009

Rupees in Billions	Attock Refinery Limited	National Refinery Limited	Pakistan Refinery Limited	Bosicor Refinery Limited	Pak Arab Refinery Limited
					US$1 = PKR82
Overdue Amounts Due from Pakistan State Oil	10.4	7.3	12.8	3.9	19.6
Financial Charges	1.3	1.4	1.8	0.6	6.3
Total	11.7	8.74	14.6	4.5	25.9
Price differential claims					
Price Differential Claim Due from the Government	2.3	0.7	0.3	21	1.6
Financial Charges	0.4	0.3	0.1	–	0.5
Total	2.74	1.0	0.4	21	2.1

Source: Company Annual Reports, 2009.

EXHIBIT 10

CASES IN MANAGEMENT PRACTICES 175

COMPONENTS IN CALCULATING THE SELLING PRICE OF PETROLEUM PRODUCTS IN PAKISTAN

Consumer prices in Pakistan were made up of the following elements:

- Ex-refinery price was based on concept of 'import parity'

- Government levies (excise duty and petroleum development levy)

- Inland freight

- Distributor and dealer margins

- Sales tax

The Ministry of Petroleum has approved the pricing mechanism. Each of the above elements has been explained below:

EX-REFINERY PRICE: The ex-refinery price of a product, which is paid to local refineries, equates to the landed cost of the product. In other words, it relates to the import parity price of the product if the same were to be imported. The base price relates to the relevant product's FOB [freight on board] price averaged for the fortnight as quoted in the Arab Gulf region to which are added other elements, like freight, duties, L/C [line of credit], and bank charges, custom duty, wharf age, etc. to arrive at the refinery price.

GOVERNMENT LEVIES: Government levies are the prerogative of the Government and are fixed in accordance with the needs of the Government. Petroleum products are an important source of any Government's revenue and Pakistan is no exception.

INLAND FREIGHT: Inland freight is used to equate the prices of the products all across Pakistan. In order to do this:

29 core depot locations have been identified and prices are kept constant over these locations.

The product wise cost of product transportation from refineries or imports to these 29 locations is allocated to the respective product and is called primary transport cost.

Primary cost represents actual cost and does not include any profit element for the marketing companies.

The cost of transporting product from these aforementioned core 29 depot locations to the respective retail outlet is called secondary transport cost and varies in accordance with the distance of the retail outlet from the nearest depot. This cost is over and above the maximum ex-depot sale price determined by the Oil Companies Advisory Committee[22] (OCAC) for the 29 core depot locations.

DISTRIBUTOR AND DEALER MARGINS: The Government fixes the distributor and dealer margins, which represent the profit element for the oil marketing company and their dealers. These margins are represented as a percentage of the Maximum Ex-Depot Sale Price. From July 2002, these have been fixed at 3.5 per cent for Oil Marketing Companies and 4 per cent for dealers.

SALES TAX: Sales tax is the last element in the consumer pricing and is calculated at 15 per cent of the price before.

Source: Oil and Gas Regulatory Authority

---

22 OCAC was an organization devoted to provide centralized reporting and advisory for the different oil companies in Pakistan.

EXHIBIT 11

CASES IN MANAGEMENT PRACTICES 177

U.S. DOLLAR PAKISTANI RUPEE EXCHANGE RATES

Change in PKR/USD Parity during FY 2009

Month End	Closing Rate (Rs)	Monthly Change in %	Change since July 2008 %
Jul-08	71.46	–	–
Aug-08	76.48	−7.02%	−7.02%
Sep-08	78.16	−2.20%	−9.38%
Oct-08	81.47	−4.23%	−14.01%
Nov-08	78.83	3.24%	−10.31%
Dec-08	79.10	−0.34%	−10.69%
Jan-09	79.10	0.00%	−10.69%
Feb-09	80.00	−1.14%	−11.95%
Mar-09	80.51	−0.64%	−12.66%
Apr-09	80.53	−0.02%	−12.69%
May-09	81.17	−0.79%	−13.59%
Jun-09	81.46	−0.36%	−13.99%

Source: State Bank Annual Report, 2008–09.

EXHIBIT 12

QUARTERLY PROFITS OF PAKISTAN'S OIL REFINERIES, 2009

Time Period	Price of Crude Oil at Period End Date US$	in millions of Pakistani rupees				
		Attock Refinery Limited	National Refinery Limited	Pakistan Refinery Limited	Bosicor Refinery Limited	Pak Arab Oil Refinery Limited
Year ended 30 Jun. 2008		2,007	6,005	2,111	15	13,383
July–Sep. 2008 Peak price	US$141	(870)	(91)	(1,390)	(2,510)	3,077
Oct–Dec. 2008	US$36	(368)	(702)	(2,587)	(5,408)	(2,500)
Jan–Mar. 2009	US$51	1,712	1,646	308	(1,210)	987
Apr–Jun. 2009	US$71	(68)	680	(903)	(1,209)	(813)
Year ended 30 Jun. 2009		406	1,533	(4,572)	(10,333)	751
July–Sep. 2009	US$65	(553)	678	(672)	(1116)	506

Source: Company Annual Reports, 2009.

2.3 PAK ELEKTRON LIMITED— CONVERTING SYSTEMS TO ERP

CASE HIGHLIGHTS AND KEY POINTS

The Pak Elektron Limited was a very large manufacturer of consumer home appliances, large distribution and power transformers, and switchgears for the power companies in Pakistan. From 2007, the company had started a process to change the information systems of the company which had become outdated.

The case presents the situation in the fourth quarter of 2011 after the Phase 1 of the implementation of the ERP Project had finished in December 2010. The company had decided in March 2011 to dispense with the services of the consulting firm supporting the implementation of the ERP Project. The main reason was that the company was facing liquidity crises and had to save costs even though there was not enough corporate knowledge developed of Oracle EBS procedures, which was the ERP system being implemented. The staff was not comfortable with the ERP system and would not let go of the old 'legacy' systems, and as such the project was in dire straits. Hence the remarks of the General Manager Finance at the opening paragraph of the case were reflecting this situation that needed special attention.

The critical item and most interesting information of the case is in Exhibit 4, which is a listing of software systems. The students with substantive knowledge of accounting systems should be able to decipher that in this company there were approximately one hundred application systems called 'legacy systems', which was extremely unusual, especially the use of multiple systems for the same functional areas. A long list of these is deliberately included in the Exhibit as this shows a number of interesting management issues. The reason given for so many systems is also stated that the company had a diverse set of activities and sales were handled in a variety of ways. The company software development section had developed systems by division or by type of business, etc so that there was more than one receivable or payable system. This showed the following aspects of management:

1. Management did not know enough about IT and it had no control on software development.

2. There were silos of information within the company as each department handled their business quite separately and by using the software, that they did, it reinforced the corporate culture of solo flight.

3. Management did not consider IT to be an enabler of profits but as a back office function as the CFO was the organizational head of the IT section as well. Also, the qualified CIO had only been hired as the company wanted the ERP system, Oracle EBS, to be implemented.

This phenomenon of multiple systems for business functions was to plague the new ERP system and almost cause the failure of Oracle EBS within this company.

POTENTIAL USES OF THE CASE

The case can be used in the following courses:

1. Management Information Systems:

   Many companies were investing in ERP systems and the case shows that simply buying a Tier 1 ERP did not ensure success; as implementing ERP software well could be very difficult. There is data in the case of the changes that were needed in IT systems and staff and how these would impact the organization. Oracle EBS was a world leading ERP but in PEL it was facing difficulty in being implemented as the staff were not adequately trained, keeping in mind their background and the work ethic in PEL. The sequence of implementing a large number of modules is discussed as it can make the difference between success and failure. All the activities were to be handled under stressful conditions as the company faced an unexpected short term cash flow crisis soon after the project started. The risk in ERP implementation needs to be factored in as the company was facing the situation after a heavy investment in acquiring the ERP system software.

2. Human Resource Management:

There are a number of HR issues that can be discussed:

1. Planning for change in technology to be used, the new skill set required for the new ERP.

2. Dealing with the fact that as a tier 1 ERP was being introduced, the salary levels of new IT staff would be higher than existing IT staff.

3. Managing the old employees who were required as a large number of legacy systems would continue to be used.

4. Training needs of the IT staff and the users.

A theme that underlies this case is that there were a lot of HR problems and it is fair to say that the issues were handled very poorly: from planning new skilled people, to handling existing staff who were required, as there were to be a large number of legacy systems in use for the foreseeable future.

3. Change Management:

    The company was using in-house developed mostly single user applications and the reader will note that there is an unusually long list of 'legacy applications'. If the reason given in the case is explored, it becomes clear that the company's management control on software developers was weak. Different department managers had developed software for departments and not the company as a whole e.g. Account receivables had separate software for power division, appliances division, generators, and generator parts. The problem that arose was that when the ERP Accounts receivable was to be implemented there was no single set of parameters. There were as a result silos of information as each department was using software solutions more or less independently within the company. The task of changing the systems and convincing people to forget their system to adopt a new system was very difficult and a lot of effort would be needed.

LEARNING OBJECTIVES

1. Identify factors to be considered to achieve value from an ERP system.

2. Evaluate the impact on department staff when a technology change is made.

3. Identify the mistakes made by the company in handling the IT staff, the training needs that were not met.

4. To understand the dynamic nature of the Software industry.

5. To understand why ERP systems are difficult to implement.

6. To see how important it is that senior management is well versed in IT.

ASSIGNMENT QUESTIONS

1. What should be included in a plan to revitalize the ERP project by Ahmed?

2. Evaluate the implementation procedures adopted and how these could be improved? What do you think could have been done differently?

3. What problems were faced by the company in adopting the system?

4. What were the objectives of investing in an advanced ERP solution?

5. Do you think the choice of Tier 1 ERP was the correct choice?

6. What inference can be drawn by looking at Exhibits 4, 5 and 6 regarding PEL management?

7. Why was the MMS software so important?

CASE TEXT: PAK ELEKTRON LIMITED: CONVERTING SYSTEMS TO ERP

On 12 October 2011, Syed Mohsin Gilani, the general manager finance of Pak Elektron Limited (PEL), was in a meeting to discuss the cash flow situation of the company with Manzar Hassan, the chief financial officer (CFO). During the discussions, he commented on the new enterprise resource planning (ERP) systems: 'Data is being input by the data entry personnel, but reports still need to be adjusted in Excel, as before. The quality and timeliness of data is a major issue for processing the information in most areas.' Salman Rehmatallah, the chief information officer (CIO) had earlier told Hassan that:

> With the wide range of legacy applications still being used, most of the users were not ensuring the accuracy of the data being entered in the Oracle EBS system, resulting in the need for reconciliation and corrections. Focus was also required on standardizing the reporting requirements and the quality of input data.

Hassan had felt for some time that the company needed to improve its information systems. The systems in use could not give accurate information quickly, as a number of reconciliations had to be made manually to ensure completeness. In 2007, he had initiated a project for a team of finance staff to analyze the available ERP software solutions for PEL to consider using. With the growth and popularity of the use of ERP systems by companies worldwide and the trend towards integration of the applications being operated across the company, the ERP Project was revived in mid-2009, and a decision was made to buy the Tier 1 ERP known as Oracle eBusiness Suite (Oracle EBS). This system had been in implementation by PEL and consultants A. F. Ferguson & Co since February 2010, and progress had been much slower than expected.

Iftikhar Ahmed, who joined PEL in September 2011 as the new financial controller, was given the task of streamlining financial reporting, which would require inculcating a culture of real time data entry. After taking over the new role, Ahmed said, 'I have five years experience of working with SAP and I shall make a plan to streamline the usage of Oracle Financials.[1] The first and foremost discipline required is to recognize the transaction on a daily basis.' He added, 'But I need support as there are technical issues, team development and re-training needs as well as other issues.'

BACKGROUND

PEL had been set up in 1956[2] by Malik Brothers in Lahore, Pakistan with the technical collaboration of M/S AEG of Germany (AEG) to manufacture transformers, switch gears, and electric motors for the power industry. AEG, however, left in the early 1960s. In 1978, PEL was taken over by the Saigol Group of companies, which were run by well-known businessmen. PEL's new distribution transformer manufacturing facility[3] started commercial production in January 2011. This new factory built on Ferozepur Road, 20 kilometres from the company's existing location, manufactured new generation transformers under a technical licence agreement from Pauwell Belgium. This licence enabled PEL engineers to receive support in designing the transformer plant, machinery selection, and layout,

---

1 The group of modules—General Ledger, Accounts Payable, Accounts Receivable, Cash Management and Assets—was known as Oracle Financials.

2 www.pel.com.pk/news.html, accessed 16 November 2011.

3 PEL Annual Report 2008, accessed 16 November 2011.

product design, training of manufacturing and design personnel, and developing operating procedures and quality control in the plant's initial years. This new factory would not only modernize and upgrade PEL's existing distribution transformer manufacturing capabilities, but would result in product innovation and production and cost efficiencies, resulting in an improved product with world-class design and technology to meet local as well as international requirements.

PEL had expanded considerably and was the second largest appliance maker in Pakistan; its shares had been traded on all three Pakistan stock exchanges since 1988. PEL also represented a variety of international brands who had appointed the company as their sole distributor for appliances such as air conditioners, refrigerators, and deep freezers. The company was organized into two main operating divisions: Power and Appliances. Exhibit 1 shows the performance of the two divisions. PEL was one of the major electrical power equipment suppliers to companies in both the public and private sectors (see Exhibit 2). Since the power products were mostly made to order, there could be a wide variety of sizes and designs on the manufacturing floor at any point in time. The appliances division consisted of facilities where various household items were manufactured (see Exhibit 3).

INFORMATION SYSTEMS AT PEL

The Legacy Solutions

The software applications used in PEL were a mixture of mostly in-house developed stand-alone and some multi-user applications. These applications were user-determined for the business process requirements of the department and were not used company-wide. Although PEL had purchased an American packaged software system known as SBT back in 2002, only two of its modules—SBT General Ledger and a limited functionality of SBT Inventory—had been implemented.

Over time, various departments within the company had automated their respective business processes and these applications had evolved in isolation, so that by 2009 there were about 100 different systems being used (see Exhibit 4). The reason for so many systems had ostensibly been the independent operations of business units that had diverse production operations, which included assembly line operations, custom fabrication, project oriented installations, indenting, and commissioning business. The two divisions handled sales differently: power division sales were in response to government tenders and had to comply with government regulations; the appliances division had a different procedure to handle its consumer sales. Application software had evolved without following any standards and patchwork was necessary to connect the two systems wherever any integration was required.

Software was developed as various departments asked for custom-made features based on their specific requirements and personal preferences. Integration of the various systems was seldom included in their design or, if available, was in a very rudimentary form. As suggested by Exhibit 4, to get accurate information for the inventory across the organization, one would have to pull information across systems being run by different departments.

Thus, there were multiple versions of business information systems for each functional area, and these did not accord to any common standard or design. Consolidating all these requirements into a unified process and a single system would be a difficult task. This was a major factor in not using the SBT software that was purchased in 2002. This freedom of operating in silos, the department-specific requirements, and the processing of accounting information in piecemeal to be uploaded to the general ledger (GL) were the major reasons for moving to an ERP and closing the legacy applications. The manufacturing processes were batch oriented, and the in-house developed material requirement costing system (MRCS) was used just to track job costs and arrive at the cost of inventory consumed. MRCS was fed quantitative and financial information by the purchasing and import management systems.

Legacy Processing

The various sources of data entry in the GL are shown in Exhibit 5. For each subsidiary system, a set of journal entries was prepared manually. Until this data was entered, the GL did not contain any meaningful information. Exhibit 6 shows that reporting for sales tax required data to be extracted from five different accounts receivable systems. This meant that the same data was being handled twice: it was first entered in the in-house developed stand-alone systems from which it was then extracted into Excel; in some cases, an extract routine may have been built to extract the data. Multiple systems with a variety of structures increased the possibility of incomplete or erroneous data being used. These multiple systems for the same application had resulted in most management reporting being 'Excel based'. This Excel based reporting not only provided the flexibility to format and realign data, but had created a culture where no one took responsibility for the data or data reconciliations and different versions of information were presented for the same data. The data was not centralized and was also subject to manual handling in Excel, which made it susceptible to errors being unnoticed.

Human Resource

Prior to the induction of the CIO, the information technology (IT) department was headed by a manager who had grown within the organization and had mainly a systems development background. In 2009, there were approximately 40 IT staff members, including analysts, junior programmers, a help desk, and user and network support personnel. The training of software personnel in Pakistan in early 2000 was very basic as only short courses in various software development packages were commonly available and these did not include any analysis of business concepts. Universities were just starting to offer four-year graduate programs in computer science. Shorter courses were popular among students who wanted a career in computer programming.

The effort to recruit staff with Oracle EBS knowledge had begun as soon as the selection of the ERP was made. A new CIO, Salman Rehmatallah, and a dedicated ERP manager, Atif Ameen, were hired. Rehmatullah had extensive experience with IT operations and had worked on multiple ERP implementations for large companies. Ameen was a chartered accountant with experience in implementing systems as a user while working in a large dairy company, and as a consultant with A.F. Ferguson & Co. Ameen was hired with the understanding that he would initially be deployed in IT and after the implementation of financial modules, would subsequently be transferred to the accounts department, he joined in December 2009, and Rehmatullah in February 2010. After the implementation of Oracle Financials[4] in December 2010, Ameen moved to the finance department to take over the role of manager, but he left soon after. Because of cash constraints, his replacement in IT was deferred for a later time, and it was decided to proceed with existing resources. His resignation rendered a gap in the ownership of the project within the finance department.

---

4   The modules known as Oracle Financials were General Ledger, Accounts Payable, and Accounts Receivable.

Based on his prior experience, Rehmatullah soon realized that there was a shortage of staff with the skills needed to maintain the new ERP system. As Oracle products were more complex than products on Visual Foxpro, which was the platform of all the legacy systems, a different set of skills was required to run Oracle EBS for the management of the database, development, and application/functional areas. Additional roles for each area were identified for which additional staff would be required. By June 2010, three new people had been hired to strengthen the Oracle resources. Additionally, staff would later be required to manage the development, maintenance, and upgrade of the Oracle EBS modules, whenever upgrades were available; this skill set was totally new and different from the existing resource skill set available at PEL.

At the same time, resources continued to be required to maintain the long list of legacy applications, only some of which were to be gradually phased out. There was a need to retain staff with Visual FoxPro knowledge to support the old systems. In 2007, Microsoft had stopped supporting Visual FoxPro, discontinuing new versions and promoting other products in the .net environment. This obsolescence of technology made it difficult to find suitable replacements for staff who left PEL. To cater to this obsolescence, internal training was undertaken to ensure that there would be staff who had diversified skill sets and could manage all the environments: Visual Fox, .net environment and Oracle. See Exhibit 7 for the revised IT department organization chart.

The complete change to a new systems platform created uncertainty, and a number of experienced staff left the company. Various factors that caused the departure of skilled IT staff included:

1. cash flow problems within the organization;

2. increase in demand by local software houses for developers; and

3. change in the skill set requirement.

The high turnover of IT staff, while providing an opportunity to hire fresh blood with multiple skill sets, coincided with the CIO's extended absence from Pakistan for personal reasons, and this impacted the development work in progress. The total staff level in the IT department had fallen from more than 40 in December 2009 to around 32 by July 2011.

This decrease, coupled with the planned changes in the IT application landscape, required hiring new staff with the capability of generating information that the standard Oracle EBS reports did not cover. Rehmatallah remarked, '2011 has been a year of recruitment, replacement, and jelling in the IT team at PEL. Out of 32 staff, 15 have been replaced in 2011 alone!' Hiring of new staff generated another problem: those with the skill set to operate Oracle commanded a higher salary than that of existing staff. Thus, change in salary structures and skill set requirements also caused some of the old staff to leave.

IT Infrastructure

The network configuration (see Exhibit 8) had 24 servers in the server farm consisting of IBM and DELL machines. These were production workhorses supporting various applications; tape devices were used for backup. Due to the lower computational power required and the practice of setting up separate servers for different applications, all of the servers were single processor machines irrespective of the technology that could support multiple processors.

The new operating system was to be Oracle Linux. Cash flow constraints had restricted spending in all areas, and this applied to acquisition of new hardware as well. Only essential new equipment was purchased, such as servers for Oracle applications and the Oracle database. The Oracle database itself required a large amount of space and memory resources to function properly, and a new Storage Area Network (SAN) was set up to provide it. The size of legacy system data for five years on the Microsoft SQL Server and Visual FoxPro was 200 gigabytes. Unlike the single file server used for the in-house developed systems that used SQL Server, Oracle had two:

1. Oracle Database Server: for one year (July 2010 to June 2011) data was approximately 200 gigabytes.

2. Oracle Application server: for the same year, data was 100 gigabytes.

Rehmatullah had forecast that the total data size of 300 gigabytes would grow to 500 gigabytes in one year's time if all modules were implemented. He felt that the current storage capacity had the space to handle this expanded volume. Consequently, to handle such large data—especially to generate intelligence reports—very heavy-duty and fast servers were needed. In May 2010, the server hardware was upgraded by adding an HP Blade server and a second SAN was set up. Because of the frequent shut downs by the public power utility, two 20 kilovolt amperes uninterruptible power supply (UPS) units were installed in parallel, in addition to redesigning and upgrading the existing power supply and monitoring system to support the data centre's operations.

PEL had sales offices and warehouses in approximately 25 locations across the country. The communication link with these locations was of various kinds:

1.   Linked by a leased line, a visual private network (VPN) had been established;

2.   The Internet was used to transfer data; and

3.   Data files were copied and transferred by email or disk.

Since the rollout of the Oracle EBS to branches was to be concluded in 2012, these 25 locations were outside the ERP processing. All locations needed to be linked under a wide area network (WAN) using DSL or DXX topology in order to be able to update the central database at the head office online. Prior to this, branch staff would need to be trained to use Oracle EBS from each remote location. This delay in the overall implementation would mean that as the branches collected cash and until they were linked with the central database, the cash management module would not have up-to-date data for the collection accounts. All emails were handled by the central Microsoft Exchange.

NEW ERP SYSTEM

Evaluation of ERP systems

The company had started its initial inquiries into selecting an ERP system in 2007. This analysis was revived and updated in 2009 so that the final decision could be taken by that year's end. The analysis included a review of two ERP solutions and evaluation of two consultants for each of them. A final report was submitted initially to Hassan and subsequently to the project committee.[5] Extracts are in Exhibit 9.

On 23 December 2009, the project committee chose the Tier 1 ERP known as Oracle eBusiness Suite, Version 12 (Oracle EBS), and the implementer chosen was the accounting firm A.F. Ferguson & Co (AFF), one of the Oracle platinum partners in Pakistan. While selecting the ERP modules (see Exhibit 10), a decision was made to buy all of them together to achieve a significant reduction in the cost of software. AFF commenced work on Phase 1 on 1 February 2010.

PEL's chairman had taken a close interest in the ERP project, both in its evaluation and the early days of implementation. However, he and the most senior members of management had become extremely busy taking care of serious business problems. This had included extensive meetings with various company department heads to reduce internal operating costs. Discussions were held with the lending banks to restructure long-term loan repayments so as to conserve cash, as the company expected cash flow constraints in the latter half of 2010.

Oracle EBS Manufacturing Solution

The Oracle manufacturing application had four components, all of which had been purchased:

1. Discrete Manufacturing

2. Flow Manufacturing

3. Production Scheduling

4. Manufacturing Execution

Because of its cash flow problems, the company had evaluated the cost of implementing the

---

5   Company documents.

Oracle manufacturing application, that is, of setting up the entire infrastructure required to run all the modules combined. It found that it would require consultant support, new hardware, and new technical staff along with incidentals, and the cost of these amounted to a large investment. The decision was to postpone implementing the complete set of modules. However, to convert all data to Oracle as the primary system in capturing business information and eliminate the legacy applications, PEL as an interim measure decided to develop a bridge called the material management system (MMS) to work with Oracle EBS Suite.

There was a variation in the basic algorithmic way that the in-house MRCS and Oracle EBS Suite processed the inventory/manufacturing transactions. A switchover from MRCS to Oracle EBS Discrete Manufacturing could only be done at the end of the fiscal year (31 December 2011) as the history data for the full year was required to be in one system for regulatory compliance. The MMS transitional system was developed to bridge the existing process gap by providing the following features:

- Bill of materials (BOM) definition

- Job definition (in-house and vendor)

- Functionality to manage the stock issuance to and from the shop floor

- Vendor job management

- Job costing-material

- Interface the inventory stock transactions back into Oracle EBS Manufacturing

PEL Adoption of Oracle

With the postponement of Phase II, one major challenge was to replace legacy systems with Oracle systems and make the Oracle database the primary source of information. This would require building transitioning interfaces or applications to eliminate the legacy application. One major such area was the cost of inventories consumed where the procurement and stores part of the functionality was available in Oracle EBS; however, the process of issuance to shop floor and its subsequent costing had not been implemented. To bridge this gap, as mentioned above, PEL took up the project to replace the legacy MRCS with an MMS, using new development tools and architecture based on data from EBS. This was an important project since the use of Oracle Manufacturing was dependent on the use of an MMS that would act as a bridge; the transactional data would be entered in MMS from where it would be interfaced in the Oracle Inventory as the 'integration point'. As the master data would all be based on Oracle Data Structure, this initiative would also facilitate the subsequent stage when PEL revived Phase II. The designed capability of the MMS included the core functionality of the legacy application MRCS that was missing in the process chain of procurement, inventory, and material costing of Oracle EBS Discrete Manufacturing. The MMS would resolve the missing features and thereby facilitate the closure of the legacy application MRCS and associated applications being used to feed it.

However, as a result of using MMS as a bridge, some of the functionality of Oracle Manufacturing would not be available:

1. The capability to define and manage the operations and resources by shop floor.

2. The conversion cost in terms of fixed overhead would not be available by operation and resource.

3. Similarly, the integration from manufacturing job to vendor purchase order for vendor jobs and with sales order would also not be there.

4. The supply chain planning would not be available.

The planned parallel run of this new application was scheduled for the first quarter of 2012. The expected benefits would be:

1. Closing all the legacy applications (including MRCS, SBT Inventory, Cost Control System CCS, and Imports Monitoring System (IMS)).

2. Streamlining basic master data in line with Oracle EBS Master Data definition.

3. Moving all information to one basic integrated application framework, thus eliminating duplication of entry.

4. Using Oracle EBS as the primary source for capturing transactions.

5. Shifting dependency away from legacy to Oracle EBS.

6. Reducing the dependency on visual studio expertise which was an obsolete skill set found very rarely in the pool of applicants for employment.

IMPLEMENTING THE NEW SYSTEM

Methodology

The AFF proposal was to complete the implementation in just over two years, and this would be achieved in three phases. AFF started work under Phase 1 on 1 February 2010 with their team being led by Irfan Faruqui, the partner in charge of the project. Phase 1 included core accounting functions (Oracle Financials), procurement, inventory, order management, and planning modules for which AFF had deputed seven functional consultants and five technical consultants. The functional specialists did a situation analysis for business processes in each functional area to develop a functional design document (FDD) based on PEL procedures, which was converted to a functional design manual (FDM). The PEL ERP team (Exhibit 7) worked closely with the AFF consultants to provide information on the company procedures and to develop revised procedures (the FDD) under Oracle EBS. The technical consultants configured the Oracle software technical stack, uploaded initial data, and developed the customized reports as required by the functional design manual (FDM). They were also helping the PEL IT staff to understand the Oracle installation of database and application software. As all the financial modules required for the Hyperion planning and financial data quality management were not implemented, their implementation was also deferred. Phase II was to include the manufacturing modules, and Phase III was to cover the Human Resource modules.

User Training

The training provided by AFF included formal instructor-led sessions as well as hands-on work for each functional area and included the following components for each member of the department staff:

1. General presentation about the functional area and how Oracle EBS was designed.

2. Functional design manuals (FDMs) were handed out as well as training manuals.

3. Hands-on work was done in a test environment under the supervision of AFF consultants.

4. Parallel data entry was started on a supervised basis, and results were matched with the legacy systems.

By August 2010, the FDMs were mostly completed, and the AFF staff used them to prepare training manuals by changing their standard manuals to suit PEL needs. The hands-on training and implementation were started in parallel to the existing legacy systems for the five modules (Accounts Payable, General Ledger, Fixed Assets, Purchasing and Cash Management). In November, two more modules (Order Management and Accounts Receivable) were started in parallel. In December 2010, after matching the results in the SBT GL and legacy fixed assets with those of the corresponding Oracle modules, the legacy systems were closed (see Exhibit 11).

Training was targeted at the user in the respective functional departments involved in the activities of the specific module or process. After the training sessions, the users gained more familiarity by hands-on use of the systems running on a parallel basis. Rehmatallah commented, 'ERP usage is very different to how legacy applications operate. This change of mind-set and the way we operate took some staff over one year to understand the way transactions have to be processed in Oracle EBS as compared to the legacy systems. Even today, despite repeated trainings, some of the users lack an understanding of basic concepts like drilling down from the General Ledger.' The timing to start the parallel processing was convenient as 30 June was the date on which the systems were closed for month and half-year end reporting. Thus, the 1 July 2010 balances were used as opening balances for Oracle EBS.

Phase 1 Progress

Phase 1 of the implementation involved a number of modules and numerous procedural changes that needed time to be understood by the users. Data processing had become integrated so that entries in one module affected other modules, which was a drastic change from the legacy systems. In addition, there were the following to be considered:

1. Phase 1 included use of eight new Oracle EBS transaction processing modules covering the financials and order management, which would replace about 30 legacy systems, resulting in a large number of processes being redesigned.

2. There were differences between the calculation mechanics of some Oracle EBS modules and the corresponding legacy systems, e.g. inventory valuation calculations in EBS are based on the material overhead application concepts whereas in the legacy systems, the actual overheads were charged on the respective inventory transactions.

3. There were constraints imposed by the liquidity crisis facing the company as additional financing would be required to move to Phase II of the implementation.

4. The changed procedures as well as understanding the Oracle EBS operational and intelligence modules had to be fully understood and adopted by PEL staff.

In March 2011, AFF suggested to Rehmatullah that they would like to start Phase II, but the above factors led PEL management to rethink their plans. A meeting with AFF's Faruqui and the key users management of PEL was held in May 2011 to review the ERP status. As no major issues were reported by the business team, it was decided to release AFF and any new implementation and support of the existing modules would be done by PEL. Phases II and III were to be deferred for the time being and AFF would rejoin PEL once they kicked off. Later on, in subsequent internal meetings at PEL, it was decided to defer Phase II and III for a year or so.

Pace of Implementation

The parallel runs, which were initially planned for a short period, were extended substantially due to the change in the overall implementation timeline. This required users to manage two parallel systems. All the data entered in Oracle EBS was not on a real-time basis. For example, in the case of inventory, the material issuance was done at the end of the month in a monthly batch, which meant that the Oracle EBS could not provide the real-time information. The new system, being very tightly integrated in the form of processes, was entirely different to how things were done in the legacy systems. This, coupled with the financial and operational issues, also slowed down the pace. The management realizing these implications, initiated the development of an interim solution in the form of MMS to close the loop of inventory and costing cycle. Software development work by nature and the complexity of the varied manufacturing processes and practices, as well as the change of core master data structures required time to conclude. These solutions were the implementation phase and were expected to be concluded by the first quarter of 2012, which would make Oracle EBS the primary source facilitating real-time information.

While the ERP implementation was in progress, unexpected changes in the business operations caused the management to make major structural changes such as:

1. Arrangement with LG for distribution or co-manufacturing was discontinued.

2. The dealership of Carrier air-conditioning expired.

3. The appliance business operating structure was changed.

All these changes also had an impact on the configuration of the Oracle EBS, and this added more complexity, which slowed down progress.

With the resignation of Ameen in February 2011, ownership and leadership to provide ERP understanding was missing in the financial area. This gap was filled in September 2011 with the hiring of Iftikhar Ahmed, who had an accounting and systems background and who, in addition to financial reporting, was made responsible for solving the bottleneck in the Oracle EBS implementation.

Ahmed was aware that nothing could be achieved unless the recording process was streamlined on a daily basis. His first task was to inculcate a culture of recording, reviewing, and reconciling the effects of the transactions immediately after entering the data. He had to carefully remind all the users that if the data was entered correctly he was confident that Oracle EBS would give the correct results. On enforcing this discipline, he soon identified the reasons for duplicate entries: transactions had not been reviewed while recording.

After Ahmed's hiring, the EBS implementation started to gain some momentum. He had already reviewed the various accounting data of Oracle Financials and found that many accounting transactions had not been posted in the respective ledgers; that most of the financial reporting was focused on the periodic review rather than detailed daily data entry and reconciliations of the accounts. There were 250 customized reports and more than 120 financial statement generator reports. Focus was also required in standardizing the reporting requirements as well as the quality of data.

ERP Benefits

By October 2011, it had been more than one and a half year since the start of implementation work by AFF, but the objectives for the main end users of Phase I, such as Gilani in the finance department, were not being met. While the external consultants (AFF) had concluded their work and had handed the full operational responsibility to PEL, the problem of using Excel to generate final reports was a major issue that had the potential to erase any benefit of the system. AFF had adopted the normal software project implementation strategy, starting with the modules that were relatively easy to implement (the Oracle Financials). However, the environment of numerous legacy systems at PEL had slowed down the implementation so that when AFF left, only a handful of legacy systems were closed (see Exhibit 11).

The initial plan was that by the end of December 2010, after six months of parallel operations, the legacy systems related to Phase 1 were to be stopped. By virtue of multiple legacy systems still being utilized and some of the core functionalities not being covered in the implemented Oracle EBS modules, the organizational tendency was to rely more on Excel reporting. The differences in the reports from the new and the old systems had to be removed before a complete changeover could be made. These differences were due to missing functionality in the new system or difference in the accounting basis and controls between the two systems. The differences notwithstanding, Rehmatallah had also discussed with the CFO that unless the legacy modules were discontinued, the staff would not attempt to adopt the new system.

CONCLUSION

Oracle E-Business Suite was designed to work as an integrated system in which information passed from one application to another without any incremental integration costs. While Oracle's applications were integrated, they were also modular, but due to PEL business constraints, the implementation of further modules was delayed. The Oracle business intelligence systems and the transactional systems used the same data and information; there was no need for changing data or any manual delay possible, whereas in the legacy systems Excel based reporting was not reliable. But for the intelligence modules to work, the transaction processing modules had to be implemented. No ERP could generate meaningful results unless information was captured on a real-time basis and the respective departments took ownership of the data.

Ahmed had set his objective clearly: to streamline the Oracle Financials modules by resolving the daily list of problems reported to the IT department by the users and ensuring a discipline that financial information was captured and reconciled on a daily basis. However, he also needed management support as it was a major challenge for him to convince his team to convert to treating the data on their personal machines as being 'live' and up-to-date. Handling the conversion from the legacy single dimension data generated in silos to an integrated relational data structure based on globally accepted business processes was the major challenge for PEL.

PEL DIVISIONAL AND CONSOLIDATED PERFORMANCE SUMMARY

DIVISION	POWER			APPLIANCES		
	Half year	Full year	Full year	Half year	Full year	Full year
Segment performance	2011	2010	2009	2011	2010	2009
Net Revenue	2,015	8,320	8,386	4,407	9,207	7,386
Profit (loss)	(295)	136	166	(343)	87	191

Balance Sheets	CONSOLIDATED As at 12/31/2010	Rupees in millions As at 12/31/2009
Capital & Reserves	4,566	4,187
Surplus on revaluing fixed assets	4,163	4,374
Long-term liabilities	7,796	7,183
	16,524	15,744
Net current assets	2,543	1,661
Long-term assets	13,981	14,083
	16,524	15,744

Source: Company files.

EXHIBIT 2

CASES IN MANAGEMENT PRACTICES 201

SALES MIX (IN UNITS) OF POWER DIVISION, 2009

Power Generation/ distribution companies	Power Transformer (MVA)	%	Distribution Transformer (MVA)	%	Switch Gear (Nos)	%	Energy Meters (Nos)	%
Public Sector	1,295	96	625	57	2,104	22	443,824	99
Private Sector	54	4	472	43	1,942	78	4,483	1
Total for 2009	1,369	100	1,097	100%	4,046	100	448,307	100

Abbreviations: MVA – mega volt amperes; Nos – numbers.
Source: Company files.

MARKET SHARE—APPLIANCES PRODUCTS

Company Name	Air Conditioners Tonnes	%	Refrigerators/ Deep Freezers Cft	%	Television Nos	%
Dawlance	82,200	34	5,460,608	52	-	
PEL	28,585	12	3,156,604	30	-	
Cool Waves	17,940	7	1,567,190	15	-	
Haier	112,000	47	505,450	3	68,000	100
Total Production	**240,725**	**100**	**10,284,006**	**100**	**68,000**	**100**

Cft: cubic feet; Nos – numbers.
Source: Company files.

EXHIBIT 4

CASES IN MANAGEMENT PRACTICES 203

LEGACY SYSTEMS LISTING

No	Project/Software Name	Development IDE	Phase
1	Accounts Payable	Visual Studio 2003	Phase 1
2	Accounts Receivable System – Power Division (PD)	Visual Studio 2005	Phase 1
3	Accounts Receivables System – Appliances Division (AD)	Visual FoxPro- VFP	Phase 1
4	Accounts Receivables System – Corporate Marketing Department (CMD)	VFP	Phase 1
5	Accounts Receivables System – Generators	VFP	Phase 1
6	Accounts Receivables System – Generator Parts	VFP	Phase 1
7	Accounts Receivables System – Parts AD	VFP	Phase 1
8	Accounts Receivables System – Power Division	VFP	Phase 1
9	Accounts Receivables Yearly Aging System	VFP	Phase 1
10	Aging Process Utility for SIS AR Web	Visual Studio 2005	Phase 1
11	Annual Manpower Requisition Plan	Visual Studio 2005	
12	Asset Management System	Visual Studio 2003	Phase 1
13	Asset Management System (Leasing)	Visual Studio 2003	Phase 1
14	Asset Management System (Unit II)	Visual Studio 2003	Phase 1
15	Attendance Services Unit I	Visual Studio 2005	
16	Attendance Services Unit II	Visual Studio 2005	
17	Automated Meter Reading	Visual Studio 2005	
18	Bank Guarantee System	Visual Studio 2005	
19	Borrowing Schedule System	Visual Studio 2005	
20	Budgeting System	Visual Studio 2003	
21	Capital Expenditure Proposal	Visual Studio 2005	
22	Capital Work in Progress	Visual Studio 2005	
23	Cheque Transactional System	Visual Studio 2005	
24	Cheque Management System	Visual Studio 2005	
26	Contracted Workshop System	Visual Studio 2003	
27	Costing Control System	VFP	
28	Courier Receiving and Dispatch System	Visual Studio 2005	
29	Corporate Services Department (CSD) Merger Software	VFP	
30	CSD Software – Area Offices	VFP	
31	CSD Software – Head Office	VFP	
32	Customer Care Management	Visual Studio 2005	
33	Customer Care Management	Visual Studio 2005	
34	Daily Routine Test	Visual Studio 2005	
35	Dies and Module System	Visual Studio 2005	

36	E-Library	Visual Studio 2005	
37	Employees Cost Management	Visual Studio 2005	
38	Employees Training Management	Visual Studio 2005	
39	Employees Training Management	Visual Studio 2005	
40	ERP Portal	HTML	
41	Final Settlement Process	Visual Studio 2005	
42	Finished Goods Inventory System (Accounts) – AD	VFP	
43	Finished Goods Inventory System (Accounts) – PD	VFP	Phase 1
44	Finished Goods System	Visual Studio 2005	Phase 1
45	General Ledger – Inquiry.	VFP	Phase 1
46	General Ledger – SBT	VFP	Phase 1
47	HR Policy Portal	HTML	
48	HR Survey	Visual Studio 2005	
49	HSE Portal	HTML	
50	Human Resource Management Web	Visual Studio 2005	
51	Human Resource Management	Visual Studio 2003	
52	Imports Monitoring System	VFP	
53	Internship System	Visual Studio 2003	
54	Inventory Control System	Visual Studio 2003	Phase 1
55	Inventory Control System (Barcode Appliances)	Visual Studio 2005	Phase 1
56	Inventory Control System (Barcode Appliances) WEB	Visual Studio 2005	Phase 1
57	Inventory Control System Power	Visual Studio 2005	Phase 1.
58	IR Portal	HTML	
59	International Standards Organization(ISO) – AD Portal	Visual Studio 2005	
60	ISO – PD Portal	Visual Studio 2005	
61	IT Labs for Punjab Government	Visual Studio 2005	
62	IT Tech Portal	Visual Studio 2005	
63	Maintenance Monitoring System	Visual Studio 2005	
64	Maintenance Monitoring System	Visual Studio 2005	
65	Manager Car Benefits Scheme	Visual Studio 2003	
66	Mobile Billing System	Visual Studio 2005	
67	Materials Requirement Costing System (MRCS)	VFP	
68	My Portal (Pay Slip)	Visual Studio 2005	
69	Payroll – (Staff & Workers)	VFP	

EXHIBIT 4 (CONTINUED)

CASES IN MANAGEMENT PRACTICES 205

70	PEL Address Book	Visual Studio 2005
71	PEL Dealers Survey	Visual Studio 2005
72	PEL Lucky Draw System	Visual Studio 2005
73	PEL WEB Site	HTML
74	PEL Portal	HTML
75	Performance Appraisal Sr. Staff & Management	Visual Studio 2005
76	Personnel – Overtime	VFP
77	Personnel – Staff	VFP
78	Personnel – Workers	VFP
79	Power Monitoring System/Order Tracking System	Visual Studio 2003
80	PRAL Data System	Visual Studio 2003
81	Procurement and Inventory Module	Visual Studio 2005
82	Production Planning System	Visual Studio 2005
83	Production Tracking System	Visual Studio 2005
84	Provident Fund – GL	Visual Studio 2005
85	Quality Control System	Visual Studio 2005
86	Recruitment Management System	Visual Studio 2005
87	RED Automation System	Visual Studio 2005
88	Sales & Inventory System AR Web	Visual Studio 2005
89	Sales Tax Monitoring System	Visual Studio 2005
	SBT IC Inquiry System	VFP
91	Supplier Corrective Actions	Visual Studio 2005
92	Testing Result Software for Instrument Transformer Plant	Visual Studio 2005
93	Transformer Design System	Visual Studio 2005
94	Visitor Management System	Visual Studio 2005
95	Wages hours System \ Resource & Information Management System	Visual Studio 2005
96	Wada Repair Software	Visual Studio 2005
97	Weighing Scale System	Visual Studio 2005
98	Weighing Scale System – Unit II	Visual Studio 2005

Abbreviations: LCM – Landed Cost Management; AD – Appliances Division; PD – Power Division; CMD – Corporate Marketing Department; CSD – Corporate Services Department.
Source: Company files.

LEGACY GL DATA PROCESSING

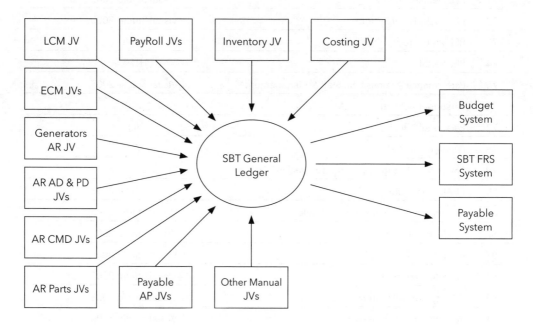

Abbreviations: JV – Journal Voucher; LCM – Landed Cost Management; ECM – Employee Cost Management; AR – Accounts Receivable; AD – Appliances Division; PD – Power Division; CMD – Corporate Marketing Department; FRS – Financial Reporting Systems.

Source: Company files.

EXHIBIT 6

CASES IN MANAGEMENT PRACTICES 207

LEGACY SALES TAX SYSTEM (STS)

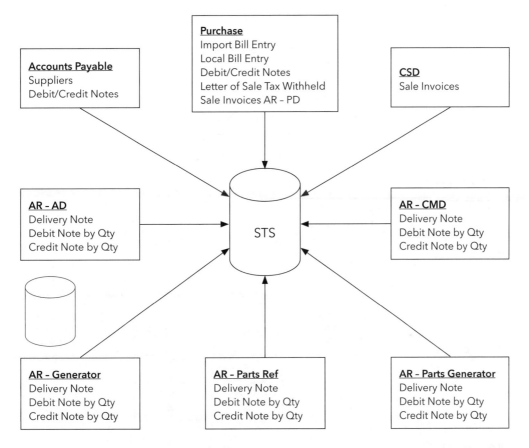

Abbreviations: AR – Accounts Receivable; AD – Appliances Division; PD – Power Division; CMD – Corporate Marketing Department; CSD – Corporate Services Department; QTY – quantity.
Source: Company files.

REVISED PEL IT ORGANIZATION CHART

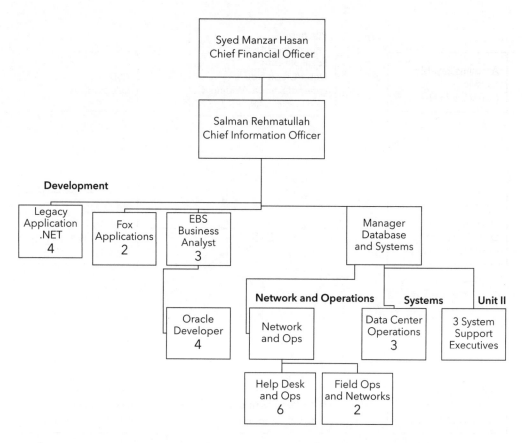

Source: Company files.

EXHIBIT 8

CASES IN MANAGEMENT PRACTICES 209

NETWORK SUMMARY

PEL Network

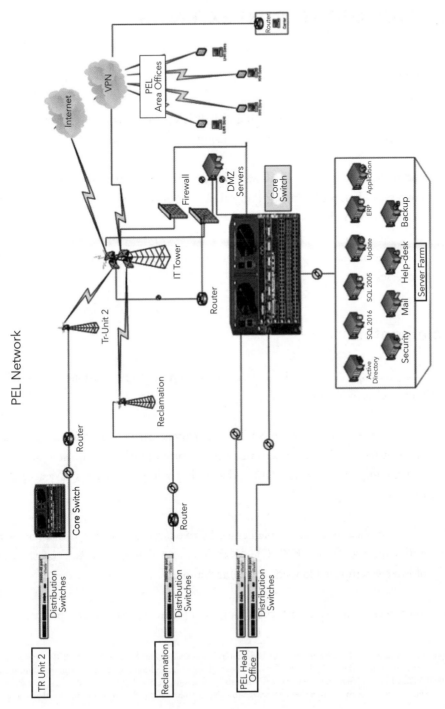

Source: Company files.

ERP EVALUATION REPORT EXTRACTS

General

1. All of PEL competitors were using Tier 1[6] ERP: Siemens, ABB, Orient, and Haier were using SAP, and Dawlance was using Oracle eBusiness Suite.

2. The decision that Tier 1 software would suit PEL was based on the diversified processes of manufacturing and sales. The only Tier 1 software supported in Pakistan was by SAP and Oracle.

3. The solution had to provide good manufacturing applications for PEL business processes.

Implementers

1. The decision to choose Tier 1 narrowed the choice to two products: SAP R/3 and Oracle eBusiness Suite.

2. There were two well-known SAP implementers: Siemens in Karachi and Abacus Consulting in Lahore. Siemens was a competitor of PEL as they also manufactured power equipment, and if awarded the work would give Siemens easy access to the internal workings of PEL.

3. Oracle applications were implemented by two large accounting firms, Taseer Hadi & Co. (partner firm of KPMG) in Karachi and A.F. Fergusons & Co. (partner firm of Pricewaterhouse Coopers- PWC) in Lahore.

4. There were many smaller firms acting as implementers of the two products.

---

6 Software classification: The software industry had various categorization mechanisms and the ERP systems had been categorized under tiers. Tier 1 was the ERP for very large multi-location and multinational operations and included SAP, ORACLE, and BAAN. Generally the turnover of the users of this software was over US$200 million. Tier 2 software was for smaller companies with turnovers between US$20 to US$200 million and with a single site and less than 200 users.

EXHIBIT 9 (CONTINUED)

CASES IN MANAGEMENT PRACTICES 211

5. PEL wanted the help of a well-known firm based in Lahore. AFF and Abacus were suitable as they had their offices in Lahore and had implemented Oracle/SAP applications in a number of locations.

Product comparison

1. As both the software were leading ERP systems, the overall solutions of both were technically acceptable and other factors needed to be considered such as:

2. The upfront cost for SAP was higher than Oracle.

3. The Oracle eBusiness Suite12 was a major improvement over version11i, the previous release.

4. SAP applications, built around their latest R/3 system, provided the capability to manage financial, asset and cost accounting; production operations and materials; personnel and plants; and archived documents.

5. AFF had experience of over 20 installations of Oracle applications including Dawlance, which was also an appliance manufacturer.

Visits to ERP installations

The PEL team, consisting of Hassan, the manager of IT and some staff, visited two installations each of Oracle and SAP and discussed the experience in implementing and operating each product. These were:

SAP sites: Atlas Honda Limited, manufacturer of Japanese motor cycles, and Packages Limited, manufacturer of packaging materials.

Oracle Applications sites: Century Paper Board Mills Limited, manufacturer of packaging materials, and Haleeb Foods, a large dairy processing company.

EXHIBIT 9 (CONTINUED)

The objective of the site visits was to satisfy Hassan and his team that the systems were able to provide localized reporting to satisfy users and on how the ERP had been implemented by the consultant involved.

Comparative analysis of two vendors each for the two ERP being considered:

Implementer of Oracle EBS: A.F. Ferguson & Co.		Implementer of SAP: Abacus Consulting	
Established	1893	Established	1987
Consultants	150+	Consultants	120
Product	Oracle applications	Product	SAP
ERP Experience	10+ years	ERP Experience	5+ yrs
Implementation methodology	Experience – AFF		ASAP – Accelerated SAP
Client list	20 installations	Client list	8 installations
Oracle – KPMG Clients	**7 installations**	**SAP – Siemens clients**	**20 installations**

Source: Determined by case writer after interviewing PEL staff on 12 October 2011.

EXHIBIT 10

ORACLE MODULES PURCHASED, RESPONSIBLE STAFF

Oracle eBusiness Suite 12i Modules purchased	ERP team of PEL		
	Appliances Division	Power Division	Common
Financials: Accounts Receivables Accounts Payables Fixed Assets Cash Management General Ledger			Amir Sattar S.M. Amir Wasim Butt Amir Turab Gilani
Order Management Advance Pricing	Amir Sattar Tariq Irani	S.M. Amir Nadeem-ud-Din	
Discrete Manufacturing Flow Manufacturing Production Scheduling Manufacturing Execution	Salman Aslam Khalid Azeem Imtiaz Ahmad Faryal Gohar Muhammad Asif Amir Sattar	Majid Shakeel S.M. Amir	
Inventory Management	Ashar Abbas Malik Naeem Ullah Salman Aslam Amir Sattar	Ashar Abbas Malik Naeem Ullah Khan Majid Shakeel S.M. Amir	
Purchasing	Shahid Tanvir Imtiaz Rasheed Mir Malik Naeem Ullah Tayyab Rasheed	Asif Hamid Imtiaz Rasheed Mir Malik Naeem Ullah Tayyab Rasheed	
Project Management Project Resource Management Project Billing Project Costing			Amir Turab Gilani Naveed Arshad
Core HRMS, Performance Management, Payroll, Compensation Management			Waqar Khadim Salman Chaudhry Ali Kamran

Source: Company files.

PHASE 1 SUMMARY

Oracle EBS Modules	Nature	Related PEL legacy systems to be replaced	No of legacy systems	Status
Oracle General Ledger	Core TPS	Budgeting system, General Ledger Inquiry and SBT General Ledger	3 systems closed	It was being used, the legacy systems were closed after reconciliation. But the discipline of reconciliation process was not maintained.
				In the last year with the operational issue, the budget was not updated in the system. The budgeting exercise is now being organized for 2012.
Oracle Payables	Core TPS	Accounts Payable Accounts Payable (Audit)	2 systems closed	After reconciliation the legacy was closed. The discipline of reconciliation was overlooked in the period and is now being reinitiated.
Oracle Assets	Core TPS	Asset Management system, Asset Management System Leasing, Asset Management System Unit II	2 systems closed	The legacy systems closed after reconciliation. Problems and balances issues with GL are being resolved.
Oracle Cash Management	Reporting		N.A	The full implementation will only be possible with complete roll out. Partially implemented for some locations.
Oracle Purchasing	Core TPS	Costing Control system, Inventory Control system PD, MRCS, Procurement & Inventory module, Supplier Corrective Action		5 System still in use
Oracle Inventory	Core TPS	Finished Goods system, Inventory Control system, FG Inventory system (Accounts) AD, FG Inventory system (Accounts) PD, MRCS, SBT IC system, Procurement & Inventory module		6 systems still in use + 1 common with Purchasing

EXHIBIT 11 (CONTINUED)

CASES IN MANAGEMENT PRACTICES 215

Oracle Business Intelligence for Procurement	Dash-board		N.A.	N.A	Implemented
Daily Financial Intelligence	Dash-board		N.A.	N.A	Implemented
Daily Inventory Intelligence	Dash-board		N.A.	N.A	Implemented

Oracle Order Management Suite					Status
Oracle Order Management	Core TPS	FG Inventory system (Accounts) AD, FG Inventory system (Accounts) PD, FG system, AR Power Div, AR Appliances Div, AR System CMD, AR system Generators, AR system Generator Parts, AR system Parts AD, AR system Power Div, AR Yearly Aging system; Aging Process Utility for SIS AR Web		12 systems still in use	Partial use as all locations not using Oracle
Oracle Receivables;	Core TPS	AR Power Div, AR Appliances Div, AR System CMD, AR system Generators, AR system Generator Parts, AR system Parts AD, AR system Power Div, AR Yearly Aging system; Aging Process Utility for SIS AR Web, Finished Goods Inventory system Accounts AD, Inventory system Accounts PD, Finished Goods system, Sales & Inventory system AR web		13 systems still in use and 6 common with orders	In process of replacement, will only be replaced completely after roll-out to all locations
Oracle Shipping Execution	Core TPS	FG Inventory system (Accounts) AD, FG Inventory system (Accounts) PD, FC System		3 systems in use common with receiv-ables	In process of replacement, will only be replaced completely after roll-out to all locations

Daily Customer Fulfillment Management Intelligence	Dash-board	N.A.	N.A	In process of replacement, will only be replaced completely after roll out to all locations.
Daily Shipping Intelligence	Dash-board	N.A.	N.A	In process of replacement, will only be replaced completely after roll out to all locations.
Oracle Hyperion Budgeting and Planning Suite		**Purpose of Hyperion**		**Status**
Oracle Hyperion Planning Plus	Reporting	Querying and reporting	N.A	Deferred until the above Financials are error free
Oracle Financial Data Quality Management	Reporting	Querying and reporting	N.A	Deferred until the above Financials are error free
Total 16 Oracle modules 7 Transactions Processing TPS, 3 Reporting, 5 Intelligence and 1 Asset Manager			Total 33: 7 legacy systems closed 26 still in use	Data reconciliation discipline and streamlining real time process is essential to generate value from the modules implemented. The roll-out to all locations would facilitate the closure and consolidation to one platform.

Abbreviations: AR – Accounts Receivable; AD – Appliances Division; PD – Power Division; CMD – Corporate Marketing Department; CSD – Corporate Services Department; FG – Finished Goods; MRCS – Material Requirement Costing System; Unit II – new factory.
Source: Determined by case writer after interviewing PEL staff on 12 October 2011.

2.4 MODERN AGRICULTURAL FARM— BUDGETING FOR CONTROL

CASE HIGHLIGHTS AND KEY POINTS

Jehanzeb Alamgir was one of the partners and a joint owner of the 448 acre farm called Modern Agricultural Farm located in the Sindh province in the south of Pakistan. He was actively involved in managing the farm, and in May 2011 had initiated a project to upgrade the performance management system of the farm. This was to improve control of the head office in Lahore about 850 miles from the farm and to evaluate the achievements each year. The main revenue generating items were the mango fruit orchard, the fodder crops of maize, barseem, and the main crops wheat and cotton. While the 225 acres of the orchard had trees, it was possible to cultivate and grow crops in the land between the trees also. The portfolio of items to be grown was one that could maximize the contribution each year but had to meet a number of conditions. The operations of the farm were subject to many risks which needed to be considered and any potential for loss minimized.

Jehanzeb had decided in 2011 that the systems for performance evaluation at the farm would be similar to what was in corporate entities. He had acquired a software, Sage Pro ERP, for use in the financial management of the farm. To enable better control the farm area available of 448 acres had been divided into blocks of 8 acres each called Managed Units (MUs).There were about 60 MUs whose performance was to be tracked, some area of the farm was still not cleared for planting. Jehanzeb had decided that the systems for performance evaluation at the farm would be similar to those used in the other businesses of the group.

Hashim, a management analysis and research consultant had been advising Jehanzeb on the changes to be made to develop systems and procedures. Hashim had suggested various changes in processes during the last ten months of the project. The main change had been that he had stressed that an annual Master Budget Plan (MBP) covering all the MAF activities be established to control operations.

The decision paragraph on page 1 states what was required from the student: Jehanzeb wanted to ask Hashim to look into the pattern of receipts during the RABI season of the current year to identify a way to reduce the incidence of cash shortages. He also wanted help to prepare an MBP for the next year with the changes that he considered to avoid cash shortages. A lot of material is given in the case that relates to the constraints in terms of water, soil, fertilizer, disease control, and pesticide use.

TEACHING OBJECTIVE AND TARGET AUDIENCE

The case is suitable for courses in management accounting and control that focus on cash flow and budgeting.

The case can be used at the undergraduate level to teach the methodology of developing an operating budget. It can also be taught to an introductory postgraduate class in which a higher level of analysis will be required to examine the risk factors in farming.

The case does not require detailed accounting knowledge, but students should have some experience in the use of Microsoft Excel in business.

TEACHING OBJECTIVES

1. To prepare the cash flow for the year in the statutory format and to determine how the cash available can be sheltered from fluctuations (see Exhibit TN-1).

2. To make a risk analysis by evaluating the variables of each crop's output that affect farm income.

3. To determine how the farm should select the portfolio of crops to maximize the contribution margin and thereby its profit.

4. To prepare a budget for the year ending May 2012.

LEVEL OF DIFFICULTY

The students, especially those who have not worked in a finance department, may have difficulty in understanding the various Excel files, which are effectively the books and records of the farm for the period being considered.

The case has a lot of qualitative data, and the instructor can address various risks faced by the farm as a profit maximizing business entity.

ASSIGNMENT QUESTIONS

1. With the help of a graph, explain the situation faced by the farm as regards cash balances and how this can be resolved.

2. Prepare the budget for 2011–2012 from the data and explain how this helps to improve control on farm operations.

CASE TEXT: MODERN AGRICULTURAL FARM: BUDGETING FOR CONTROL

In May 2011, Jehanzeb Alamgir, a director in the Alamgir Group of businesses and the managing partner of Modern Agricultural Farm (MAF), was reviewing the set of performance reports for the previous month sent in by the farm accountant. These reports had been designed by the consultant Hashim Ahmed, who was working on a project to make the MAF systems compatible with those of other Alamgir Group companies. The next project meeting was to be held during the last week of May. On recommendation by Ahmed, a master business plan (MBP) for 2011 had been developed for the first time by MAF, and Alamgir felt that Ahmed's help would be needed to develop the plan for 2012.

Alamgir was looking for a way to handle the fluctuations in MAF's monthly cash flow. He had selected the Rabi season that had just finished to analyze the situation. Recently, he had wanted cash to purchase farm animals but had found that the required amount was not available. In an earlier meeting with Ahmed, Alamgir had said,

> My manager sells an acre of maize fodder at Rs. 30,000 with my consultation. He prepares the sales order [in fact, there was no formal sales order]. When I run short of cash, I learn that he had collected the money and used it at the farm for some farm work and reported it later, although he had no right to do that!

Ahmed, a management analysis and research consultant, had been advising Alamgir on improving performance reporting and management control. The main change, he stressed, was to establish an annual MBP to control operations. Alamgir had earlier acquired computer-based accounting software from SAGE Pro, which he thought would be helpful in expediting accounting and reporting. He was now committed to implementing an overall operating controls framework based on zero-based annual budgeting. This would help to enable improvement in farm output by setting new performance indicators. Training in preparing various reports had been provided earlier to the farm accountant.

FARM BACKGROUND

MAF was located in the province of Sindh in the south of Pakistan, about 850 kilometres from Lahore where the Alamgir Group had its head office. The farm area was a total of about 448 acres[1] and used canal water for irrigation. Some of the land was shale, and another 100 acres had not been cleared for use. The farm workers were generally unskilled labourers provided by a contractor during the harvest of cotton and wheat. The full-time staff who remained on site included the farm manager and the two workers (called *baildars*) who watered the crops and security guards; the accountant lived in Agriabad, a nearby town. There were also attendants in the rest house where the partners or other visitors to the farm stayed.

The agricultural year in Pakistan was split into two seasons: Rabi and Kharif. The Rabi crops, harvested in March and April, were known as the 'winter crop'. The term Rabi means 'spring' in Arabic. The major crops of the season were wheat, cotton, gram, lentil, onion, potato, sunflower, canola, and barley. The Kharif crops were harvested in October and November as the Kharif sowing season started on 1 May and continued till 30 October. Some crops were usually sown with the beginning of the first rains in August, the southwest monsoon season. The term Kharif means 'autumn' in Arabic. Major Kharif crops were cotton, sugarcane, millets (bajra and jowar), paddy (rice), maize, moong (pulses), groundnut, red chili, and soybean. The two seasons formed the performance year for MAF—in this case, from 1 November 2010 to 31 October 2011.

The choice of crops to be grown in each season was dependent on many factors: suitability of the weather and soil, the current cash flow situation, the length of time the crop needed to mature in the field, the contribution margin that was likely to be achieved, and the likelihood of the finished crop needing storage before dispatch. Keeping this in view, MAF planned to grow the main crops of wheat, cotton, maize fodder, and sarson (mustard) during the 2011 Rabi season and to grow cotton, maize fodder, jawar, and sunflower in the Kharif season.

---

1   1 hectare = 2.47 acres, Document1, www.pakissan.com/english/allabout/crop/wheat/index.shtml, accessed 4 March 2013.

MAIN CROPS

Wheat

Wheat was the main staple food item of Pakistan's population and the largest grain crop in the country.[2] Planting of winter wheat took place from mid-September through October, and it was harvested from mid-May through June. Being a worldwide cultivated grass, wheat grain was a staple food used to make flour for leavened, flat, and steamed breads, as well as biscuits, cookies, cakes, breakfast cereal, pasta, noodles, and biofuel. It had a long growing period of about 10 months from sowing to harvest. Wheat was planted to a limited extent as a forage crop for livestock, and the straw could be used as fodder for livestock or as a construction material for roofing thatch. At MAF, wheat was planted late; since some fields were sown in January, some proceeds of the sale of the wheat planted in fall 2010 were outstanding at an amount of Rs. 1.7 million,[3] which was to be received in May 2011. The contribution based on the price of Rs. 21 per kilogram was Rs. 4,436 per acre.

Cotton

Cotton,[4] which was also known as 'white gold,' was an important crop in Pakistan and many developing countries. The crop yield was dependent on the environment in which it was grown and the land use polices of the cropping system adopted by MAF management. Alamgir was very conscious of this and regularly obtained advice from agronomists. The different crops each year were rotated in the two seasons to protect the nutrient value of the land. Factors responsible for stagnant cotton production included excessive rain at the time of sowing, high temperatures at the flowering stage, late wheat harvesting resulting in less area for the cotton, incidence of leaf curl virus and soil system, and weather adversity. The input costs had to be closely monitored at MAF, and for this a good cost accounting record was required.

The cotton was sold to ginneries at the international price of phutti, as the freshly picked produce was called. All the proceeds for the sale of cotton had been received. The sale terms

---

2   www.pakissan.com/english/allabout/crop/wheat/index.shtml, accessed 7 March 2013.
3   US$1= Pak Rs. 87.5.
4   www.pakissan.com/english/issues/why.cotton.is.problematic.crop.shtml, accessed 7 March 2013.

were delivery against cash. The phutti price was dependent on the international trend of cotton prices. There was thus an uncertainty factor as to what the ultimate price was likely to be for the MBP for the following year. The contribution based on the prevailing price of Rs. 90 per kilogram was Rs. 41,150 per acre.

Sunflower

Sunflower,[5] grown for edible oil, was one of the four most important annual crops in the world. In Pakistan, its seed contained 35 to 55 per cent oil content. Research work on this crop had shown that there was great potential for growing it under all soil and climatic conditions, in rain fed and irrigated farming systems as well as in different agro-ecological zones. It was grown in some areas of the province of Sindh, where the spring crop was sown in February or July and harvested in May or October.

Sunflower in Pakistan was mainly grown to extract edible oil, and the fact that the crop was ready for harvest between 90 and 110 days after sowing made cropping management easier. For MAF the flexibility in the time when it could be grown was important as Alamgir thought that this crop, if planted at the correct time, could generate cash in the lean period. The contribution of sunflower at the prevailing price of Rs. 22 per kilogram was Rs. 4,436 per acre.

FODDER CROPS

Pakistan had a large stock of farm animals, including buffaloes and cows for milk production and goats and sheep for meat. There was a stable and regular demand for fodder to feed these animals. Most of the animals were in rural areas; in the recent past, large numbers of buffaloes and cows had been raised by dairy farms to supply milk to processing plants.

---

5   www.parc.gov.pk/1subdivisions/narccsi/csi/sunflower.html, accessed on 5 March 2013.

Sarson (Mustard)

Sarson, grown as fodder for farm animals, had a three-month maturity period and was sold for cash. This was another crop whose cultivation could be strategically timed so that it was harvested to generate cash when required. Sarson was produced in very small quantities as it was sensitive to variations in weather. This created a demand for other crops such as maize, jowar, and oats. MAF was aiming to expand the scope of MBP to identify strategic products, such as a variety of fodder crops, to benefit from such market imbalances, and wanted to establish a mechanism to do so.

Also, like other Pakistani farmers, Jehanzeb wanted to increase the production by utilising technology efficiently. To increase profitability, it was necessary to improve fodder supply through enhanced production practices and also to reduce the growth of weeds. Although herbicide use had become popular, the weeds still stayed for some time, which affected output adversely. Besides mustard, there were other products that could be used as animal feed. The new items needed further analysis by MAF as the contribution of mustard based on the prevailing price of Rs. 318 per kilogram was Rs. 4,532 per acre per cut. The number of cuts of a fodder crop, from 1 to 6, could affect the actual contribution realized.

Maize (Corn)

The setting up of a very large maize processing plant in the province of Punjab had improved the prices realized by farmers. This plant, located near Faisalabad, produced starch, glue, and other farm animal feed products. As this one plant had a huge demand, the sale of maize was not a problem. However, the crop was susceptible to insect attack, which could reduce production substantially.

MAF cash needs meant that its main fodder crop was maize and that it had to keep the fields sprayed to protect the plants from the insect called borer. By May 2011, the three cuttings for the Rabi season had been completed and the balance of the crop was expected to bring cash receipts of Rs. 0.4 million. The contribution based on the prevailing price of Rs. 9 per kilogram was Rs. 27,010 per acre.

Barseem (Clover) and Guar (Pea)

These crops were sown from September to November and harvested from mid-December to May; up to five or six cuttings could be achieved from one crop. These fodder crops were planted in a small area and, when ready, were sold for cash—this helped the farm cash flow in March when cash receipts were low.

Barseem that was sown from April to September was harvested from June to December, while guar was sown from April to July and harvested from June to December. Generally, the conversion of the fodder crop into cash took only four to six months from the date of planting. The contributions based on the prevailing prices of Rs. 8 per kilogram for barseem and Rs. 19 per kilogram for guar was Rs. 37,207 per acre and Rs. 176,238 per acre, respectively.

SOIL REJUVENATION

Jantar (Sesban) and Guar

These two plants were required to fill the space between crops as the main source of green manure. When ready, they were ploughed back into the land to replenish the soil with the nutrients eroded by growing crops.

The prominent cropping systems (the order in which the crops were grown) in Pakistan were:

1. rice-wheat

2. cotton-wheat

3. mixed cropping (sugarcane, maize, wheat, cotton)

4. oilseed-pulses-wheat.

The first three cropping systems were very exhaustive, and the soil became weak in nutrients.

Over the years, farmers had experienced that the use of nitrogen- and phosphate-based fertilizer was harmful as the soil yields declined. To remain close to a natural solution, MAF used major green manure crops, as discussed above.

FRUIT

Mango

The mango[6] orchard covered a very large area, about 225 acres, and was also the major revenue generator for MAF. Most of the trees (3,500) that produced fruit had been planted many years ago. Another 600 were young saplings planted during the last three years.

Mango Tree Management

A variety of mango adaptable to the climatic conditions and the environment was the foundation on which mango tree management systems[7] were built. An adaptable variety was one that, under specific climatic conditions, showed regularity of bearing and high productivity of good quality fruit. Different varieties of fungi and insects attacked and killed mango trees; the relationship of insect and disease was a complex one but was manageable through the use of proper fertilizers, cultivation, and integrated disease management practices, which combined fungicides with suitable insecticides. The use of fungicides increased the cost of production and also decreased the fruit quality because of their toxic substance residues. The trees were regularly treated by MAF from January to March.

The irrigation system was one of the most important resources in a commercial orchard. The type of irrigation system depended on the capital budget for orchard development. MAF was using the old flood system and realized that each year the amount of canal water available was reduced. Therefore, they would need to invest in a sprinkler system that used much less water.

---

6   www.pakissan.com/english/allabout/horticulture/mango.tree.mortality.shtml, accessed 7 March 2013.
7   www.shanthap.tripod.com/mb1.htm#unde, accessed 6 May 2013.

The large size of the garden made it the major focus of farm activity during harvest time. The trees started to flower in February and early March, and the fruit ripened during June and July. Once the fruit ripened it had a very short shelf life, so the produce had to be plucked in a semi-ripe stage. Some of the fruit fell from the trees and was damaged so could not be sold in the regular market. To prevent this from happening, the fruit was taken off the tree by a special cutter tied to the end of a long pole that cut the end of the branch to which the mango was attached. The market for mangoes was of two kinds: the ripe fruit was sold at an attractive price as it was considered the 'king of fruits' in Pakistan, and the damaged ones were bought by beverage companies to prepare products from the juice.

Methods of sales of mangoes were of two types: either the harvesting of the entire orchard was contracted out, or the farm could sell the fruit itself. The sale contract was signed after the bidder made an estimate of the fruit on the trees and made a bid. This was negotiated by the farmer; among other terms, the agreement included a payment schedule. Normally, payment was received in three installments: one-third was payable in advance, one-third after a certain quantity had been harvested, and the final third on completion of harvest but before the last truck was dispatched.

Sales in 2011 were to be handled in-house, and for this, trucks had to be arranged to deliver to the dealers in Lahore whose market (known as a 'mandi') was the largest in Pakistan and set the prices for the whole country.

The MBP contained the budget for the mango orchard and was a simple document that was based on the output and prices of last year increased by a factor of 12 per cent (see Exhibit 1).

Other Fruits

The farm also had a few other fruits useful in generating cash. These included 300 guava, four acres of banana, 50 lychee, and 400 jamun. The banana trees brought in handy cash, while the number of the other trees was not of a commercial size, so their fruits were either sold or consumed during the year.

VEGETABLES[8]

Onion was one of the key condiments used in all households all the year round in the cooking and preparation of meals in Pakistan. International research also suggested that onions in the diet might play a part in preventing heart disease and other ailments. Onions, which could be planted either in July and August or in November, took three months to mature. The other vegetables grown were sweet potatoes and chili. Vegetables required daily inspection and were labour-intensive as they had to be harvested and delivered to the wholesale market as soon as they ripened; thus, only a small portion of land was cultivated with vegetables.

FARM OPERATIONS

The cropping plan and how the land was to be used were prepared by Alamgir at the head office in consultation with the farm manager (see Exhibit 2). The MAF land had been split into equal sized subunits, called 'managing units' (MU), consisting of about eight acres each. Two irrigation canals were nearby, one on either side of the land boundary. The quantity of farm irrigation water was sanctioned by the government irrigation department and was in limited supply. The farm was managed onsite by a resident farm manager who kept in close contact with Alamgir and was expected to carry out the work in accordance with the annual budget. Variances from the budget were to be explained in an analytical report.

Management Control

The MBP was prepared from a base of zero for all produce except mangoes and was to serve as a benchmark to determine the year's performance. The cost collection system was designed to run under Sage Pro software and would collect costs by MU, the basic land unit for performance reporting. The farm manager was in charge and was assisted by a farm accountant who was responsible for recording daily transactions and all financial

---

8   www.pakissan.com/english/allabout/horticulture/vegetables/onion.shtml, accessed 23 April 2013.

reporting. Guidelines for accounting and recording transactions had been provided in the form of standard operating procedures.

In the rural economy of Pakistan, business dealings were mainly in cash, and some of the amounts handled at the farm could be very large. As a method of control on cash, Alamgir had established two bank accounts in Agriabad, one in the name of the farm and one in the name of the local partner, H. Bashir. The funds were sent from head office to Bashir's account, from where they were given to the farm in cheques as required by the farm manager. All receipts of sales, which were mostly cash, were also deposited in the Bashir account. There were approximately 30 support staff who carried out watering, security, hoeing, and working at the rest house.

The flow of various accounting control documents had also been established and inventory controlled by using standard documents to record the various processes followed. The documents were designed to be used for data entry once the Sage Pro software was implemented. Inventory was classified on receipt and stored in one of three stores: chemicals, finished product, and fertilizer. At harvest time, the record of output was kept according to MU so that the yield for the crop could be established, since yield per acre was a key performance measure. The Sage Pro software had been installed at the head office, and data entry for all transactions was done by the accountant at the farm via remote link to the system in Lahore. The four modules to be used were to handle inventories, receivables, payables, and general ledger accounting.

The farm accountant sent his working papers monthly to head office. The effort to prepare a budget had raised the issue of cost accounting, since the variable unit costs and individual components of farm operations had to be analyzed with the revenues to achieve an acceptable margin on sale. Cost accounting for the farm was needed to provide the detailed cost of input, which was also required to prepare the budget. An initial effort had been made by the accountant, whose statistics were used to prepare the MBP.

Alamgir planned to review the cash receipts, which were dependent on the portfolio of products grown, with Ahmed. The planting and type of crops could be changed to take care of monthly expenses. This would require an iterative procedure to determine what combination of crops would maximize the total contribution margin.

Variety	Number of trees	Area in acres	2011 Production	2011 Revenue
			kgs	Rs in 000
Sindhri	1,692	93	130,200	5,773
Deasee	782	43	11,000	264
Chaunsa	657	37	36,100	2109
Dusehri	171	9	13,500	702
Langra	271	15	14,000	539
Ratol	62	4	700	23
Saroli			14,500	173
TOTAL	3,635		222,000	9,771

Source: Farm records.

EXHIBIT 2

CASES IN MANAGEMENT PRACTICES 231

RABI season				KHARIF season		
Item	Number of cuts	Area in acres	Used twice	Item	Number of cuts	Area in acres
M-Fodder	1	31.00		Sunflower	1	44.03
M-Fodder–3 cuts	3	27.00	27	Cotton	1	40.66
Onion	1	16.00		Jawar	1	44
Sarson	1	58.08		Moong	1	8
Wheat	1	44.33	16.5	Mash	1	8
Cotton	1	88.48		Cauliflower	1	3
Jantar	1	40.00	40	Maize Fodder	1	48
Subtotal		305	(86)	**Subtotal**		196
Mango		225.00		Mango		225.00
Unused		14.00		Unused		28
Total Net Acres		**448.00**		**Total Net Acres**		**448**

Source: Farm records.